ABOUT READING SUCCESS

Y0-AGJ-491

Welcome to Rainbow Bridge Publishing's *Reading Success Grade 2*. *Reading Success Grade 2* provides students with focused practice to help develop and reinforce reading skills in areas appropriate for second-grade students. *Reading Success Grade 2* uses a variety of writing types and exercises to help build comprehension, phonics, vocabulary, language, reasoning, and other skills important to both reading and critical thinking. In accordance with NCTE (National Council of Teachers of English) standards, reading material and exercises are grade-level appropriate with clear instructions to guide each lesson. Activities help students develop reading skills and give special attention to vocabulary development.

Editor . . . . Heather R. Canup
Cover and Layout Design . . . . Chasity Rice
Inside Illustrations . . . . Andy Carlson, Bill Neville
Cover Photo . . . . Images used under license from Shutterstock, Inc.

TABLE OF CONTENTS

HOW TO ENCOURAGE READING

You can help your child develop good reading habits by reading with him regularly. Reading with your child can help him acquire a lasting love of reading. Start your child's school year reading with books from the *Reading Success* Second Grade Reading List.

Share your reading experiences. Read some of the books you enjoyed when you were your child's age. Ask other friends and relatives for book suggestions. Then, share them with your child.

Visit the library. Try to find books that meet your child's specific interests. Ask a librarian which books are popular among children in your child's grade. Ask about other resources, such as stories on tape, in magazines, and on computer software.

Encourage your child to read a variety of materials. Help your child understand directions by reading house numbers and street signs. Allow your child to help you cook a meal by reading a recipe.

Show your child you like to read. Sit down with your own choice of book, newspaper, or magazine. After dinner, share stories and ideas that might interest your child from the book, newspaper, or magazine you read.

Relate reading to real life. Help your child read current events from a newspaper. Or, help your child find Internet articles about topics she is studying in school.

Schedule routine reading. Schedule time for reading several times each week. You can help your child read a book, or you can read bedtime stories on designated nights of the week.

SECOND GRADE READING LIST

Adler, David A.
Cam Jansen: The Mystery of the Dinosaur Bones

Andersen, Hans Christian
The Emperor's New Clothes

Avi
Finding Providence: The Story of Roger Williams

Barracca, Debra and Sal
The Adventures of Taxi Dog

Berenstain, Stan and Jan
The Berenstain Bears books

Bond, Michael
Paddington Bear books

Bunting, Eve
Going Home

Byars, Betsy
Tornado

Caudill, Rebecca
A Pocketful of Cricket

Delton, Judy
Pee Wee Scout books

Flack, Marjorie
The Story about Ping

Friend, Catherine
The Perfect Nest

Graham, Joan Bransfield
Splish Splash

Hegi, Ursula
Trudi and Pia

Himmelman, John
Chickens to the Rescue

Holabird, Katharine
Angelina Ballerina

Hopkinson, Deborah
Girl Wonder: A Baseball Story in Nine Innings

Ingman, Bruce
Bad News! I'm in Charge!

Johnston, Tony
The Wagon

Kimmel, Eric A.
The Chanukkah Guest

Klayman, Neil Steven
Boris Ate a Thesaurus

Komaiko, Leah
Annie Bananie

SECOND GRADE READING LIST

Leaf, Munro
The Story of Ferdinand

Levitin, Sonia
Nine for California

Lexau, Joan M.
Striped Ice Cream

Lobel, Arnold
Frog and Toad books

Mayer, Mercer
There's Something in My Attic

Paraskevas, Betty
Peter Pepper's Pet Spectacular

Rawlinson, Julia
Fletcher and the Falling Leaves

Rey, H. A.
Curious George books

Rosenthal, Amy Krouse
Little Pea

San Souci, Robert D.
Cendrillon: A Carribean Cinderella

Schwartz, David M.
How Much Is a Million?

Sharmat, Marjorie Weinman
A Big Fat Enormous Lie

Sharmat, Mitchell
Gregory, the Terrible Eater

Shefelman, Janice
Young Wolf and Spirit Horse

Small, David
Imogene's Antlers

Soto, Gary
Chato's Kitchen

Stewart, Sarah
The Gardener

Titus, Eve
Anatole

Turner, Ann
Dust for Dinner

Varennes, Monique de
The Jewel Box Ballerinas

Waber, Bernard
Lyle, Lyle, Crocodile

Wick, Walter
Walter Wick's Optical Tricks

Willis, Jeanne
Don't Let Go!

Read the poem.

I am a library, and through my door
Are shelves of books and so much more.

Through my doors, adventures are free,
So, please come in quietly.

My books can take you to outer space,
Deep into the ocean, or anyplace.

Read my books, and you will see
What the world can really be.

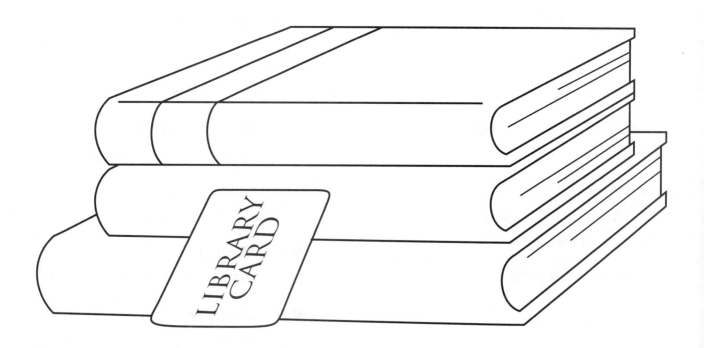

READING SUCCESS RB-904110

THE LIBRARY

Use the poem on page 6 to answer the questions.

1. Which sentence tells the main idea of the poem?

   A. Reading takes a lot of practice.

   B. You have to be quiet in a library.

   C. Library books are full of adventures.

2. According to the poem, where can books take you?

   A. to the library shelves

   B. through the library doors

   C. anyplace

3. The poem says, ". . .through my door, are shelves of books and so much more." Write an X by the things you could find in a library.

   _____ a computer   _____ DVDs

   _____ maps   _____ encyclopedias

   _____ basketball hoop   _____ a couch

Write a word from the poem that rhymes with each word. Then, think of a word of your own that rhymes.

4. door   _____   _____

5. free   _____   _____

6. space   _____   _____

7. see   _____   _____

Read the story.

Nick loves sports. No matter what the season, Nick is always playing with a ball. In the winter, he plays basketball. In the spring, he plays soccer. In the summer, he plays baseball. And, in the fall, he plays football. He is good at shooting the basketball, kicking the soccer ball, hitting the baseball, and running with the football. Nick is good at sports. He is a good sport, too, because he always tries his best and encourages his teammates.

Use the story on page 8 to answer the questions.

1. Which sentence tells the main idea of the story?

    A. Nick loves sports.

    B. Each year has four seasons.

    C. Sports are fun.

2. Draw a line to connect each sport to its season.

    soccer   winter

    football   spring

    basketball   summer

    baseball   fall

Write the base word for each word.

3. shooting   _____

4. kicking   _____

5. hitting   _____

6. running   _____

Cross out the word that does not belong in each group.

7. mitt   baseball   hoop

    bat   batting   helmet

8. hoop   basketball   free throw

    line   football   dribble

9. soccer ball   baseball   goal

    goalie   shin guards   kicking

THE SNOWMAN

Read the story.

It was a snowy day. Braxton and Hayden decided to make a snowman. They bundled up and ran outside. First, they rolled a great big snowball for the body. Then, they rolled a medium-sized snowball for the middle. Finally, they rolled a small snowball for the head. They stacked the three snowballs together. They found rocks for his eyes and mouth. They used a carrot for his nose. They used sticks for his arms. They were proud of their snowman when they finished.

THE SNOWMAN

Use the story on page 10 to answer the questions.

1. Number the events from the story in order.

   _____ They rolled a medium-sized snowball.

   _____ They found rocks for his eyes and mouth.

   _____ They rolled a great big snowball.

   _____ They rolled a small snowball for the head.

   _____ They stacked the snowballs.

Write the two words that make up each compound word.

2. snowman   _____   _____

3. snowball   _____   _____

4. pinecone   _____   _____

5. outside   _____   _____

Write the correct plural form of each noun.

6. day   _____

7. snowman   _____

8. stick   _____

9. snowball   _____

10. pinecone   _____

Read the poem.

Come to the meadow where the primrose grows
And daisies and cowslips are lined up in rows.

Buttercups look as yellow as gold;
Truly, it is a sight to behold.

Busy bees humming about them are seen.
Grasshoppers chirp in the tall grasses so green.

Butterflies happily flutter along.
The bluebirds are singing a lively new song.

So, come to the meadow, and there you'll see
Spring come alive for you and for me.

Use the poem on page 12 to answer the questions.

1. Which sentence tells the main idea of the poem?

    A. The meadow is pretty in spring.

    B. Bees are busy insects.

    C. Bluebirds like to sing.

2. What animals sing a lively song?

    A. grasshoppers

    B. bees

    C. bluebirds

3. Which of these is not a flower?

    A. buttercup

    B. butterfly

    C. cowslip

4. Draw a line to connect each pair of rhyming words.

    grows   green

    gold   rows

    seen   me

    along   behold

    see   song

Write the singular form of each word.

5. daisies   _____

6. buttercups   _____

7. butterflies   _____

TULIPS

Read the poem.

In my flower garden, tulips always grow,
Straight like soldiers all in a row.

With colors so bright, reds, oranges, yellows too,
They are one of nature's special gifts just for you.

A tulip's colorful petals are shaped like a cup
Holding little raindrops for birds to drink up.

Winds cause them to sway
Back and forth each day.

But, still my tulips grow
Like soldiers in a row.

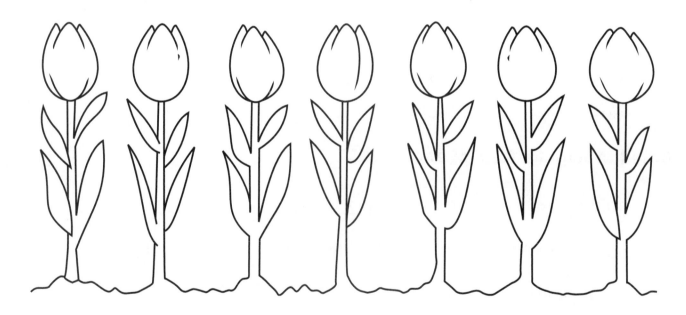

READING SUCCESS RB-904110

Use the poem on page 14 to answer the questions.

1. What is the poem about?

    A. a flower garden

    B. tulips

    C. soldiers

2. What are the tulips compared to?

    A. soldiers

    B. rainbow

    C. raindrops

Look at the index from a book about flowers. Write the page number where you could find information about each of the following kinds of flowers.

A		H I J		S	
apple blossom	37	iris	8	spring	15
aster	62	**K L**		stamen	6, 7
B		larkspur	47	stigma	6, 7
blossom	13	lily	42	summer	16
buttercup	65	**M N**		sunflower	17
C		marigold	29	**T U**	
chrysanthemum	23	**O P Q**		thistle	27
cowslip	25	pansy	31	tulip	26
D E		petal	6	**V W**	
daffodil	27	pistil	6, 7	violet	22
daisy	15	**R**		winter	15
F G		rose	19	wisteria	20
fall	30			**X Y Z**	
garden	2			zinnia	60

3. tulips _____

4. daisies _____

5. pansies _____

6. roses _____

Read the poem.

Pitter patter, pitter pat. . .
How I love the rain!

Storm clouds moving in,
The rain is about to begin.
How I love to see the rain!

Tiny sprinkles on my face,
Little droplets playing chase.
How I love to feel the rain!

I open up my mouth so wide,
Letting little drops inside.
How I love to taste the rain!

Tapping on my window,
It's a rhythm that I know.
How I love to hear the rain!

Everything looks so green,
And the fresh air smells so clean.
How I love to smell the rain!

Pitter patter, pitter pat. . .
How I love the rain!

THE RAIN

Use the poem on page 16 to answer the questions.

1. Which sentence tells the main idea of the poem?

    A. There are many reasons to not like rain.

    B. There are many reasons to like rain.

    C. Storms are scary.

2. Draw a line to connect the sense to what the author of the poem loves about the rain.

    sight   tapping on the window

    touch   storm clouds moving in

    taste   little drops inside my mouth

    sound   tiny sprinkles on my face

    smell   clean, fresh air

Find a word in the poem that rhymes with each word in the list. Write the word on the line.

3. begin   _____

4. face   _____

5. wide   _____

6. window   _____

7. green   _____

Add the suffix *ing* to each word.

8. move _____   9. let _____

10. play _____   11. tap _____

CHANGING WITH THE SEASONS

Read the passage.

Humans are not the only ones to change the way we dress with the seasons. We change our clothing with the seasons to protect us from the weather. Animals do the same to protect themselves when the seasons change. They know when it is time to change.

For example, the arctic fox has a thick, white fur coat in the winter. A white coat is not easy to see in the snow. This helps the fox hide from enemies. When spring comes, the fox's fur changes to brown. It is then the color of the ground.

The ptarmigan bird, or snow chicken, has white feathers in the winter. It, too, is hard to see in the snow. In the spring, the bird **molts**. This means that it sheds all of its feathers. The bird grows new feathers that are speckled. When the bird is very still, it looks like a rock.

Use the passage on page 18 to answer the questions.

1. What is the passage mostly about?

    A. how people change with the seasons

    B. how seasons change

    C. how animals change with the seasons

2. What color is the arctic fox's fur in the winter?

    A. brown

    B. white

    C. black

3. What happens to the ptarmigan bird in the spring?

    A. It molts.

    B. It flies south.

    C. Its feathers turn red.

4. What does *molt* mean in the story?

    A. to change colors

    B. to shed feathers

    C. to hide from an enemy

Write the two words that make up each compound word.

5. springtime   _____   _____

6. bluebird   _____   _____

7. wintertime   _____   _____

On a separate sheet of paper, write words you could type into a search engine or look up in a book to read more about how animals change each season.

Read the poem.

Sing a song of summer
with arms stretched open wide.
Run in the sunshine.
Play all day outside.

Hold on to the summer
as long as you may.
Fall will come quickly
and shorten the day.

So, play in the water.
Roll in the grass.
It won't be long now
before you'll be in class.

Use the poem on page 20 to answer the questions.

1. Which sentence tells the main idea of the poem?

    A. Enjoy summer while it lasts.

    B. Summer gets too hot.

    C. School starts in the fall.

2. What season comes after summer?

    A. winter

    B. spring

    C. fall

3. Write an *X* by each thing you can do in the summer.

    _____ play outside

    _____ rake leaves

    _____ go swimming

    _____ build a snowman

    _____ ride a bike

    _____ go to the park

Write the two words that make up each compound word.

4. sunshine   _____   _____

5. outside   _____   _____

6. raindrop   _____   _____

Read the poem.

Lemonade for sale!
Lemonade for sale!

The sun is hot.
It'll hit the spot.

We made it sweet.
It's quite a treat.

We've got lots of ice.
It's really quite nice.

It's just one dime.
You've got the time.

Try our delicious lemonade—
It's simply the best we've ever made.

Use the poem on page 22 to answer the questions.

1. Which sentence tells the main idea of the poem?

    A. Someone is selling lemonade.

    B. You need to have something to drink.

    C. Lemonade is delicious.

2. Write an *X* by each reason you should buy the lemonade.

    _____ It is sweet.

    _____ Someone is trying to earn money for a new bike.

    _____ The lemonade has a lot of ice.

    _____ You have the time.

    _____ You don't have any lemonade.

3. What does "It'll hit the spot" mean?

    A. The lemonade is just what you need when it is hot.

    B. The lemonade will spill on the right spot.

    C. The lemonade has spots in it.

Write the two words that make up each contraction.

4. it'll _____ _____

5. it's _____ _____

6. you've _____ _____

7. I've _____ _____

Read the story.

"Let's go shopping," my mom said.

"What do we need?" asked my dad.

"How about a dish for our fish?" I suggested.

"But, we don't have a fish," said my dad.

"How about a wig for our pig?" suggested my little brother.

"But, we don't have a pig," said my dad.

"How about a hat for our cat?" suggested my big sister.

"But, we don't have a cat," said my dad.

"How about a log for our dog?" suggested Mom.

"We don't have a dog," said my dad.

"It seems to me," said my mom, "that what we need is a pet."

So, we went shopping for a pet.

Use the story on page 24 to answer the questions.

1. What did the family decide they needed?

   A. a dish for a fish

   B. nothing

   C. a pet

2. Write who said each sentence.

   A. Who said, "How about a hat for our cat?" _____

   B. Who said, "What we need is a pet"? _____

   C. Who said, "But, we don't have a fish"? _____

   D. Who said, "How about a wig for our pig?" _____

3. Draw a line to connect each pair of rhyming words.

   dish   cat

   wig   dog

   hat   fish

   log   pig

Quotation marks (" ") **are used to show the words that someone says. Put quotation marks around what is being said in each sentence.**

4. Let's go shopping, said Mother.

5. Can we buy a pet? asked my brother.

6. We don't need a pet, said my father.

7. That dog needs a home, said my mother.

8. Okay, said my father, we can buy the dog.

Read the poem.

Have you seen my cat?
Yes, I've seen your cat.

Really? My cat is big.
I saw a big cat.

My cat has spots.
I saw a big cat with spots.

My cat's spots are black.
I saw a big cat with black spots.

My cat runs fast.
I saw a big cat with black
spots running fast.

You did see my cat!
Where is it?
I don't know.
I saw it last week.

Use the poem on page 26 to answer the questions.

1. Draw a line to connect each word with its opposite meaning.

   big   black

   solid   slow

   white   spots

   fast   little

Circle the missing short vowel in each word.

2. My cat has sp__ts, it is not solid.

   a   o

3. My cat is b__g, not little.

   a   i

4. My cat runs f__st, not slow.

   a   i

5. My cat is bl__ck, not white.

   a   o

Read the information inside the box to answer the questions.

LOST CAT
Big black cat with spots
Please call Rachel at 555-0123.
REWARD

---

6. What is the poster about? _____

7. Whom should you call if you find the cat? _____

8. What number should you call? _____

Read the poem.

I wonder if animals have dreams.

Does a fish dream of swimming in the sky?
Does a bird dream of flying in the ocean?

I wonder if monkeys dream of learning in school
While children dream of swinging from vines.

Or, maybe worms dream of being as big as snakes,
And snakes dream of having legs like a centipede.

I wonder.

Use the poem on page 28 to answer the questions.

1. What does the author wonder about?

    A. if monkeys wish they could go to school

    B. if animals have dreams

    C. if animals are happy

Write _T_ for the things that are true. Write _F_ for the things that are false.

2. _____ Fish swim in the sky.

3. _____ Monkeys swing from vines.

4. _____ Snakes have legs like centipedes.

5. _____ Birds fly in the sky.

Write the base word for each word.

6. swimming   _____

7. flying   _____

8. learning   _____

9. swinging   _____

10. being   _____

11. having   _____

Read the story.

There was a swamp in the jungle.

Five wild pigs tromped by. "It's hot!" they squealed. So, into the swamp they went.

Four monkeys came swinging by. "It's hot," they chattered. So, into the swamp they went.

Three frogs hopped by. "It's hot," they croaked. So, into the swamp they went.

Two snakes slithered by. "It's hot," they hissed. So, into the swamp they went.

One big crocodile wriggled by. "It's not hot," he grinned, showing his great big teeth, "but I am hungry." So, into the swamp he went.

Suddenly, out from the swamp came two snakes, three frogs, four monkeys, and five wild pigs. It didn't feel so hot anymore.

Use the story on page 30 to answer the questions.

1. Why did the animals get out of the swamp?

   A. They weren't hot anymore.

   B. It was too crowded.

   C. So the crocodile wouldn't eat them.

Synonyms are words that mean the same or almost the same thing. Cross out the word in each row that is not a synonym of the other words.

2. said   yelled   asked   kicked

3. jump   roll   hop   leap

4. cried   laughed   giggled   chuckled

At the top of each page in a dictionary are two *guide words*. The guide word on the left tells you the first word found on the page. The guide word on the right tells you the last word on the page. Circle the word that would be found on the page with the following guide words.

5. **patter—penguin**

   panda   pig   paw

6. **match—monkey**

   moan   magic   motor

7. **crocodile—cross**

   crow   crop   crush

8. **bear—buffalo**

   bunny   bat   bison

Read the story.

My dog, Eli, loves to go to the river. Every Saturday morning, I take Eli to the park by the river to play. The first thing Eli does when we get there is run down to the water.

Eli likes to splash in the water. The cold water doesn't bother him. When he gets out of the water, he shakes and shakes. I stand back so that the water does not get on me. Then, he looks for a rock in the sun to take a nap on. He sleeps there until I whistle for him when it is time to go home.

I think our Saturday trips to the river are something that Eli looks forward to all week.

Use the story on page 32 to answer the questions.

1. Which sentence tells the main idea of the story?

   A. Eli takes a nap.

   B. Eli loves the river.

   C. Eli is a good dog.

Circle the missing short vowel in each word.

2. I have a d___g.

   i   o

3. Eli likes to spl___sh in the water.

   a   i

4. Eli finds a rock in the s___n.

   u   a

5. Eli n___ps on the rock.

   i   a

Words in a dictionary are listed alphabetically. Number each set of words in alphabetical order from 1 to 5.

6.		7.		8.	
_____ splash		_____ thing		_____ love	
_____ stand		_____ take		_____ look	
_____ shake		_____ think		_____ lake	
_____ sleep		_____ then		_____ lamp	
_____ scream		_____ thrash		_____ limp	

Read the story.

My brother Juan made a birdhouse. The birdhouse was beautiful. I hung it in the front yard. The neighbors asked about our new birdhouse. This gave me an idea. Juan and I could earn money selling birdhouses.

Juan built three more birdhouses. I made posters. I put them up around the neighborhood. We charged four dollars for each birdhouse. We sold all three birdhouses the first day. Five other neighbors asked for birdhouses, too.

With my brain and my brother's birdhouses, we started our own business.

Use the story on page 34 to answer the questions.

1. Which sentence tells the main idea of the story?

   A. Everybody loves birdhouses.

   B. A brother and sister started a birdhouse business.

   C. You should put your brother to work.

2. Write an *X* by each of the ways Juan's sister used her brain.

   _____ She got the idea to sell the birdhouses.

   _____ She painted the birdhouses.

   _____ She made posters.

   _____ She made five more birdhouses.

   _____ She hung the posters around the neighborhood.

3. Draw a line to connect each present tense verb to its past tense verb.

make	built
hang	gave
give	sold
build	made
sell	hung

Divide the following words into syllables. Use a dictionary if you need help.

4. birdhouse _____

5. beautiful _____

6. business _____

Read the story.

I like to watch the birds in my garden. The robins came as the snow was melting. The male robin has a red chest. He helped his mate build a nest in the cherry tree. I peeked into the nest. I counted three tiny eggs.

Two magpies live in my garden. Their feathers are shiny black and white. The magpies built their huge nest in the pine tree. Magpies can copy the sounds of other birds. They are noisy.

My favorite birds to watch are quail. They have topknots on their heads that bob when they walk. Quail make their nests on the ground under bushes. They live in groups called **flocks**. They can run very fast. When they are frightened, they scatter to different places. When the danger is gone, they whistle to each other to come back. I love watching the baby quail follow their parents.

Use the story on page 36 to answer the questions.

1. What does the author of the story like to do?

   A. watch birds

   B. collect birds

   C. watch insects

2. Which bird is not in the garden?

   A. magpie

   B. lark

   C. robin

   D. quail

3. Draw a line to connect each bird to where it built its nest.

   A. robin   under a bush

   B. magpie   in a pine tree

   C. quail   in a cherry tree

4. What does the word *flock* mean?

   A. a group of birds

   B. a family

   C. a group of whales

Write the base word of each word.

5. peeked _____

6. watching _____

7. counted _____

8. places _____

9. groups _____

10. melting _____

Read the passage.

Animals move in different ways. Some animals move on four legs. Horses gallop on four legs. Dogs run on four legs. Lions pounce on four legs.

Some animals move on two legs. Kangaroos hop on two legs. Ducks waddle on two legs.

Some animals move through water. Some animals move in the sky. Other animals move on the ground. Fish swim in the water. Birds fly in the sky. Snakes slither along the ground.

It's fun to think about all of the different ways animals move.

WALK LIKE THE ANIMALS

Use the passage on page 38 to answer the questions.

1. Which sentence tells the main idea of the passage?

    A. Ducks waddle.

    B. Animals move in different ways.

    C. Animals are different in many ways.

2. Draw a line to connect each animal to how it moves.

horse	flies
kangaroo	swims
duck	slithers
fish	gallops
bird	waddles
snake	hops

3. Write each animal's name in the correct group. Some animals may belong in more than one group.

cat	whale	blue jay	goldfish
robin	deer	owl	penguin

    Moves on two feet   **Moves on four feet**

    _____   _____

    _____   _____

    Flies   **Swims**

    _____   _____

    _____   _____

Read the passage.

The ladybug is a very interesting insect. It is also called a ladybird beetle. Most ladybugs are red or yellow with black spots. The California ladybug's shell is yellow with black spots. The ladybug has a tiny head and no neck. Its body is round and shaped like half a pea. It can run very fast on its short legs. The ladybug's wings are tucked under its shell. It can fly very well.

The ladybug lays its eggs on the underside of green leaves. When the grubs hatch, they are very hungry. They quickly start to eat plant lice. Lice are insects that hurt plants. They can ruin a farmer's crop. Fruit growers like ladybugs because they eat harmful lice.

The California ladybug was brought to the United States from Australia. It helps protect orange, lemon, and grapefruit trees.

Use the passage on page 40 to answer the questions.

1. Where does the ladybug lay its eggs?

    A. in a nest

    B. on the underside of a leaf

    C. on the bark of a tree

2. What type of animal is a ladybug?

    A. an insect

    B. a bird

    C. a mammal

3. *Proper nouns* are specific names of persons, places, or things. Proper nouns always begin with a capital letter. Find three proper nouns in the last paragraph.

    _____   _____   _____

4. Number the words in alphabetical order.

    _____ larva

    _____ beetles

    _____ lice

    _____ grub

    _____ insects

    _____ eggs

    _____ wings

Read the passage.

Ants can be found almost anywhere on our planet. There are about 12,000 different types of ants. Ants are **amazing** insects. An ant can carry things many times its weight. Ants use feelers on top of their heads to find food.

Many ants have very sharp teeth. An ant's jaw opens sideways. Ants use their jaws to eat. They also use their jaws to carry their babies and to fight. Ants are social insects. They live in large groups called colonies.

Use the passage on page 42 to answer the questions.

1. Which sentence tells the main idea of the passage?

    A. Ants are strong.

    B. Ants are amazing.

    C. Ants have big jaws.

2. Write an *X* by each sentence that gives a detail about the main idea.

    _____ An ant can carry things many times its weight.

    _____ Ants use feelers to help them find food.

    _____ I have an ant farm.

    _____ An ant's jaw opens sideways.

    _____ Some ants were in the cupboard.

3. What does *amazing* mean?

    A. interesting

    B. able to go through a maze

    C. small

Words like *they* and *it* take the place of other words. Write the words *they* and *it* stand for in each sentence.

4. An ant is very strong. It can carry things many times its weight.

    It stands for _____.

5. Ants have jaws that open sideways. They use their jaws to eat.

    They stands for _____.

Read the passage.

Koalas live in Australia. They spend most of their time high up in tall **eucalyptus** trees. Koalas eat the leaves from the tree. They eat about two to three pounds of leaves every day. They drink very little water. The eucalyptus leaves give the koala the water it needs.

Many people think koalas are bears because they look like bear cubs. Koalas are not bears. They are **marsupials**. Marsupials are a special kind of mammal. They have pouches to keep their babies warm and safe. Koalas have pouches just like another animal that begins with a *K*. Can you guess what it is? It is a kangaroo.

THE KOALA

Use the passage on page 44 to answer the questions.

1. What is the passage about?

   A. Australia

   B. koalas

   C. eucalyptus trees

2. Where do koalas spend most of their time?

   A. in eucalyptus trees

   B. in their mothers' pouches

   C. in caves with bears

3. What is a *marsupial*?

   A. a mammal with a pouch

   B. an animal that swims underwater

   C. a mammal with a long trunk

4. What is *eucalyptus*?

   A. a type of marsupial

   B. a type of tree

   C. a baby koala

Write the plural of each word.

5. koala   _____

6. marsupial _____

7. pouch   _____

8. baby   _____

9. leaf   _____

GERMS

Read the passage.

Germs are things you should not share. Germs can make you sick. Even though you cannot see germs, they get into a body in many ways. Germs get in the body through the nose, mouth, eyes, and cuts in the skin. We share germs when we sneeze or cough and do not cover our mouths. We share germs when we drink from the same cup or eat from the same plate.

To keep germs to yourself and to stay well:
- Wash your hands with soap.
- Cover your mouth when you cough or sneeze.
- Do not share food or drink.
- Keep your fingers out of your nose, mouth, and eyes.
- Drink a lot of water.
- Get a lot of fresh air.
- Eat healthy meals.
- Get plenty of sleep.

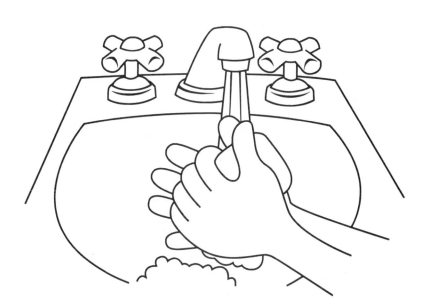

Use the passage on page 46 to answer the questions.

1. Which sentence tells the main idea of the passage?

    A. Germs are things you do not want to share.

    B. You can't see germs.

    C. Wash your hands often.

2. Write an *X* by the ways you can keep germs to yourself and stay well.

    _____ Wash your hands with soap.

    _____ Stay away from animals.

    _____ Cover your mouth when you cough or sneeze.

    _____ Get plenty of sleep.

    _____ Eat healthy meals.

3. Write *T* for the things that are true. Write *F* for the things that are false.

    _____ Germs can make you sick.

    _____ Germs get into the body through the nose, mouth, and eyes.

    _____ Cover your mouth when you cough or sneeze.

    _____ You should rub your eyes if you think you have germs in them.

Circle the missing short vowel in each word.

4. Germs can make you s___ck.

    i   o

5. Germs get in the body through c___ts in the skin.

    a   u

Read the passage.

So, you want to be a **philatelist**? If you collect stamps, that's what you are! Stamp collecting is a hobby that is fun and interesting.

If you want to start collecting stamps, you will need a few supplies. You can find these supplies at your local hobby shop. You will need a pair of tweezers. Use tweezers to move the stamps so that you do not get the stamps dirty. You will also need an album with plastic pages.

You start by collecting some stamps. The stamps you collect may be new or used. You can collect stamps from letters that arrive at your house. You can also buy special stamps to add to your collection.

Next, decide how to organize your stamps. You can organize them by their value, by the place they are from, or by a theme. Then, put the stamps in your album.

You will want to keep your stamp album in a cool, dry place away from direct sunlight. Heat, sun, and dampness can ruin your stamps.

Use the passage on page 48 to answer the questions.

1. Which sentence tells the main idea of the story?

   A. Stamp collecting is a fun and interesting hobby.

   B. You can organize stamps in many different ways.

   C. Stamps come from all over the world.

2. Write an *X* by things you need in order to start a stamp collection.

   _____ stamps

   _____ an album

   _____ a dictionary

   _____ tweezers

   _____ plastic pages

   _____ rubber gloves

3. What is a *philatelist*? _____

Write the base word for each word.

4. collection _____

5. supplies _____

6. organization _____

7. dampness _____

Read the passage.

Scrapbooks have been around for a long time. But, in the last few years, making them has become a popular hobby. What used to be a simple way of storing pictures and memories has become an art. Stores now sell scrapbook supplies. They sell special paper, special stickers and cutouts, special letters, special scissors and special albums. They also sell books about how to make scrapbooks.

Making scrapbooks is different from making photo albums. A photo album has only pictures to tell the story. Scrapbooks also include writing and **mementos** to help preserve memories.

One way to start a scrapbook is to choose a theme. The theme may be sports, school, or a vacation. Once you pick the theme, look through your pictures and mementos. Pick the ones that best tell the story you want to remember. Then, choose the paper you will use. Write something about each picture. Be sure to write the names of the people in each picture and the date that the picture was taken. Scrapbooks are a nice way to keep your memories safe.

Use the passage on page 50 to answer the questions.

1. Scrapbooking supplies sold in stores include
   A. photographs
   B. paper, stickers, letters, scissors, and albums
   C. memories

2. What does *mementos* mean?
   A. something that reminds us of what has happened
   B. something we always remember
   C. special scissors

Write the two words that make up each compound word.

3. scrapbook _____ _____

4. headline _____ _____

5. something _____ _____

6. everyone _____ _____

7. cutout _____ _____

Write the base word for each word.

8. storing _____

9. memories _____

10. supplies _____

11. organizing _____

Read the passage.

Mercer Mayer's books can be found in almost every library and bookstore. Mr. Mayer's name is on more than 300 books. He has both written and illustrated books. Some of his most popular books include *There's a Nightmare in My Closet, Liza Lou and the Yeller Belly Swamp, Just for You*, and *A Boy, a Dog, and a Frog*. Mr. Mayer likes to write about things that happened to him as a child.

Mercer Mayer was born on December 30, 1943. He was born in Arkansas. His father was in the navy, so his family lived in many different places. When he was 13, he moved to Hawaii. After high school, he went to school to study art. Then, he worked for an advertising company in New York. He published his first book in 1967. He and his wife work together on the Little Critter stories. He has two children. Now, he works from his home in Connecticut.

Use the passage on page 52 to answer the questions.

1. This passage is called a biography. Based on what you read, what do you think a biography is?

    A. a story made up about a character from a book

    B. a true story that tells about the life of a real person

    C. a short, funny story

Write *T* for the things that are true. Write *F* for the things that are false.

2. _____ Mercer Mayer is a character in a book.

3. _____ Mercer Mayer writes about things that happened to him as a child.

4. _____ Mercer Mayer lived in many different places.

5. _____ Mercer Mayer never got married.

Commas (,) are used to separate words in a series or in a date. Place commas correctly in the sentences.

6. My brother was born November 15 2001.

7. I like to eat pizza popcorn pretzels and pickles.

8. My favorite Mercer Mayer books are *There's a Nightmare in My Closet There's an Alligator under My Bed* and *Terrible Troll.*

9. The title of the book is *A Boy a Dog and a Frog.*

10. Mercer Mayer's birthday is December 30 1943.

TWO

Read the poem.

Two living things, blowing in the wind.
One stands straight, the other bends.

One is a strong tree growing tall.
The other is grass ever so small.

Both are Mother Nature's gift.
The tree you can climb. On the grass, you can sit.

Green is their color, brought on by the spring.
Grass or trees, they both make me sing!

Use the poem on page 54 to answer the questions.

1. What two things is the poem comparing?

    A. the grass and a tree

    B. a tree and a flower

    C. the wind and the rain

2. Read each description. Decide if the words describe the grass, a tree, or both. Write an *X* in each correct column.

Alike or Different?	Grass	Tree
living thing		
stands straight in the wind		
bends in the wind		
tall		
small		
Mother Nature's gift		
you can climb it		
you can sit on it		
green in color		

Write an antonym (opposite) for each word.

3. straight _____

4. tall _____

5. stand _____

Read the story.

Chris and Will are twins. They are brothers who were born December 22. Twins that look almost exactly alike are called identical twins. Chris and Will look similar, but they are not identical twins. Chris and Will are fraternal twins. That means they were born on the same day but do not look exactly alike.

Will has curly red hair. Chris's hair is brown and straight. Chris has green eyes. Will's eyes are blue. Another difference between them is their teeth. Chris is missing his two front teeth. Will has all of his teeth, and he has braces.

Both boys like to play baseball. Sometimes, they play third base. Sometimes, they play catcher. Both of them can throw the ball well. It can be fun to have a twin.

READING SUCCESS RB-904110   © Rainbow Bridge Publishing

Use the story on page 56 to answer the questions.

1. Which sentence tells the main idea of the story?

    A. Chris and Will are fraternal twins.

    B. Chris and Will have different teachers.

    C. Chris and Will look different from each other.

2. What are the two types of twins?

    A. fraternal and maternal

    B. fraternal and identical

    C. Chris and Will

3. Read each description. Decide if the words describe Chris, Will, or both brothers. Write an *X* in each correct column.

Alike or Different?	Chris	Will
born on December 22		
curly red hair and blue eyes		
straight brown hair and green eyes		
missing two front teeth		
a good ballplayer		

4. Circle each word that has a long vowel sound.

    twin   red   base

    teeth   play   fun

    braces   Will   both

Read the poem.

My brother and I are opposites.
Believe me because it's true.

I like to read. He likes to watch TV.
I like the lake. He likes the sea.

I whisper. He shouts.
I take ballet. He is in scouts.

I am quiet. He is loud.
I am humble. He is proud.

I like the slide. He likes the swing.
I like to hum. He likes to sing.

Although we're opposites to the end,
My brother is still my best friend.

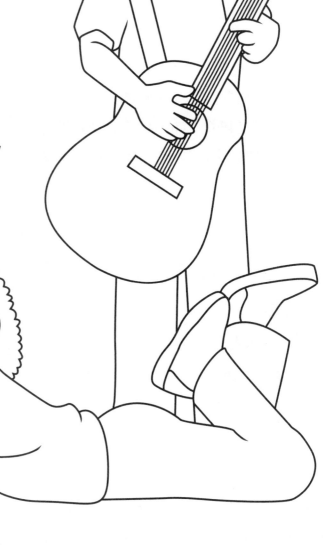

OPPOSITES

Use the poem on page 58 to answer the questions.

1. Even though they are opposites, what does the author say about her brother at the end of the poem?

    A. He is very different.

    B. He is okay.

    C. He is her best friend.

Write either the word *brother* or *sister* to correctly complete each sentence.

2. The _____ likes to read.

3. The _____ likes to watch TV.

4. The _____ is quiet.

5. The _____ is loud.

6. The _____ likes to sing.

7. The _____ likes to hum.

8. Draw a line to connect the differences between the brother and sister.

read	is in scouts
whispers	proud
takes ballet	loud
quiet	watch TV
humble	shouts

Read the poem.

I'm too old for my teddy bear,
And poor Ted is showing too much wear.

Now that I'm a bigger kid,
It's time that I kept Ted hid.

So, I said "good-bye" to my old friend
Because teddy bears are just pretend.

But that first night, I couldn't sleep
Though I tried and tried to count sheep.

I thought about my teddy bear,
Hidden in the closet there.

And now, I miss old Teddy so,
I just can't let my old friend go.

So, I tiptoed quietly out of bed
And found my little bear called Ted,

And I brought him back to bed with me.
Poor Ted still needs me, can't you see?

Use the poem on page 60 to answer the questions.

1. Which sentence tells the main idea of the poem?

   A. It's hard to give up a teddy bear.

   B. Everybody needs a teddy bear.

   C. Teddy bears are not real.

2. Why does the author feel it's time to say good-bye to Ted?

   A. He is too old for a teddy bear.

   B. He can't find Ted.

   C. Ted is in the closet.

3. Where was Ted "hiding"?

   A. under the bed

   B. in the closet

   C. in the toy box

4. Draw a line to connect each pair of rhyming words.

   bear   pretend

   kid   see

   friend   there

   bed   hid

   me   Ted

Write the two words that make up each contraction.

5. I'm   _____   _____

6. it's   _____   _____

7. couldn't   _____   _____

THE SYNONYM SONG

Read the poem.

Sometimes I talk, but other times I . . .
shout, whisper, yell, discuss, chatter, or gab.

Sometimes I walk, but other times I . . .
saunter, tromp, march, step, stroll, trudge, or trek.

Sometimes I run, but other times I . . .
skip, dash, flee, race, scramble, or scurry.

Sometimes I jump, but other times I . . .
leap, hop, spring, bound, or vault.

Sometimes I laugh, but other times I . . .
giggle, chuckle, titter, cackle, roar, or snicker.

Sometimes I sleep, but other times I . . .
slumber, rest, doze, nap, or snooze.

 READING SUCCESS RB-904110

THE SYNONYM SONG

Use the poem on page 62 to answer the questions.

1. What is a *synonym*?

    A. a word that means the opposite of another word

    B. a word that sounds like another word but has a different meaning

    C. a word that means the same or about the same as another word

2. Draw a line to connect the synonyms.

talk	dash
walk	stroll
run	chatter

Circle the best word to complete each sentence.

3. I will (whisper/shout) a secret in your ear.

4. I will (skip/dash) to get some help.

5. I will (slumber/nap) all night.

6. I (chuckled/cackled) at the comic in the newspaper.

A *thesaurus* is a book that includes synonyms of words. You can use a thesaurus to make your writing more interesting. Look at this page from a thesaurus. Then, answer the questions.

> **sad** (adj): unhappy, down, dismal, morose, miserable, cheerless, gloomy, forlorn, dejected, glum, depressed
>
> **said** (v): spoke, repeated, harped, yelled, whispered, echoed, bellowed, whined, shouted, told, sang, hammered, mentioned

7. Are the synonyms for the entry word in alphabetical order? _____

8. What does the (adj) after the word *sad* tell you about the word?

AUNT ANTONYM

Read the story.

We have a nickname for my mother's sister. We call her Aunt Antonym. She always says or does the opposite of what we say or do. At the zoo, we began at the north end of the park. My aunt began at the south end. At the monkey cage, we thought the monkeys were adorable. My aunt thought they were ugly. I said a zebra is a white horse with black stripes. My aunt said a zebra is a black horse with white stripes. At the dolphin show, we sat in the front. We like getting wet. My aunt sat in the back. She wanted to stay dry. Soon, we were hungry. My aunt was still full from breakfast. After lunch, we rode the train around the zoo. My aunt wanted to walk. Finally, my aunt said she was ready to go. We wished we could have stayed.

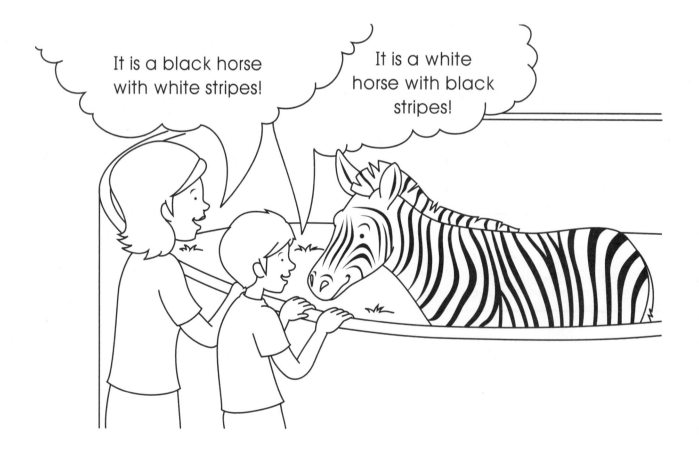

AUNT ANTONYM

Use the story on page 64 to answer the questions.

1. Why did the author call his aunt Aunt Antonym? _____

_____

_____

Write _T_ for the things that are true. Write _F_ for the things that are false.

2. _____ The author is writing about his sister.

3. _____ Aunt Antonym is the real name of the author's aunt.

4. _____ Aunt Antonym thinks monkeys are ugly.

5. _____ Aunt Antonym wanted to sit in the back at the dolphin show.

An _antonym_ is a word that means the opposite of another word. Write a word from the story that is an antonym for each word.

6. north _____   7. front _____

8. ugly _____   9. dry _____

10. black _____   11. hungry _____

Write the past tense for each verb.

12. begin _____   13. ride _____

14. think _____   15. want _____

Study the bar graph.

This year, the students at Washington Elementary want every family to join the PTA. Every class has the goal of 100% membership. Read the graph. Then, answer the questions on page 67.

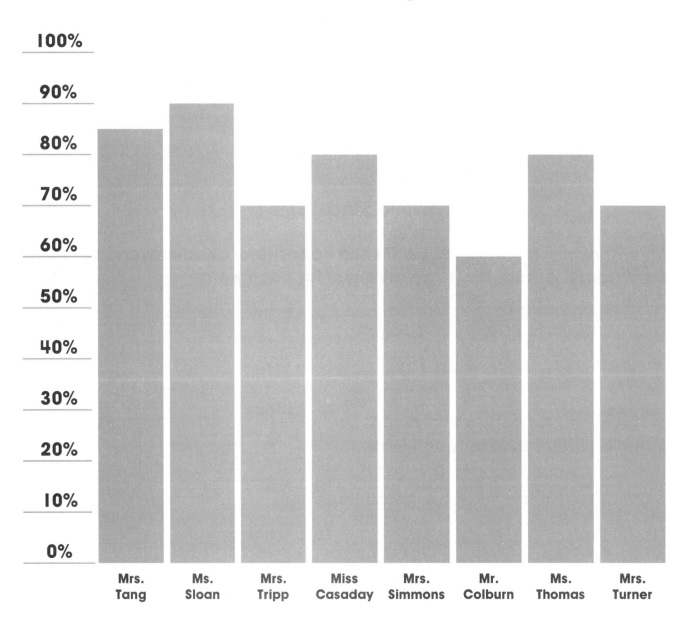

The PTA Challenge

Our Goal Is 100% Membership!

Use the bar graph on page 66 to answer the questions.

1. What is the title of the bar graph? _____

2. What is the goal of each class? _____

3. Which class is closest to the goal of 100%? _____

4. Which class is furthest from the goal of 100%? _____

5. Which two classes have reached 80% of their goal? _____

    _____

6. Draw a line to connect each abbreviation to its meaning.

    Mrs.   unmarried woman

    Mr.   woman, married or unmarried

    Dr.   married woman

    Miss   man

    Ms.   doctor, man or woman

A chart may or may not have all of the information you need. Read the questions. Circle _yes_ if the information is on the chart. Circle _no_ if the information is not on the chart.

7. Can you find out how close Mrs. Tang's class is to their goal?

    yes   no

8. Can you find out how many students are in Mr. Colburn's class?

    yes   no

9. Can you tell if Mrs. Tang's class or Mrs. Tripp's class is closer to their goal?

    yes   no

READING SUCCESS RB-904110

Read the television schedule.

Channels	7:00	7:30	8:00	8:30	9:00	9:30	10:00	10:30
Times								
2	Quiz Game Show	Jump Start		Summer the Dog			News	
4	Lucky Guess	You Should Know	Wednesday Night at the Movies *Friends Forever*				News	
5	Best Friends	Mary's Secret	Where They Are	Time to Hope	Tom's Talk Show		News	
7	123 Oak Street	Lost Alone	One More Time	Sports			News	
11	Your Health	Eating Right	Food News		Cooking with Kate		Home Decor	Shop Now
24	Silly Rabbit	Clyde the Clown	Balls o' Fun	Slime and Rhyme	Cartoon Alley		Fun Times	Make Me Laugh

TELEVISION SCHEDULE

Use the television schedule on page 68 to answer the questions.

1. What does this schedule show?

    A. times and channels of television shows

    B. times and channels of radio programs

    C. the number of people that like different shows

2. On what channels can you watch news at 10:00?

    A. 2, 5, and 11

    B. 3, 4, and 11

    C. 2, 4, 5, and 7

3. What time is the show *Silly Rabbit*?

    A. 7:00

    B. 7:30

    C. 8:30

4. What is the title of the Wednesday night movie?

    A. *Lost Alone*

    B. *Mary's Secret*

    C. *Friends Forever*

Circle the word in each row that does not belong.

5. food	cook	knit	eat
6. slime	rhyme	clown	time
7. talk	whisper	laugh	shout
8. know	guess	predict	suppose
9. funny	serious	humorous	silly

Read the flyer.

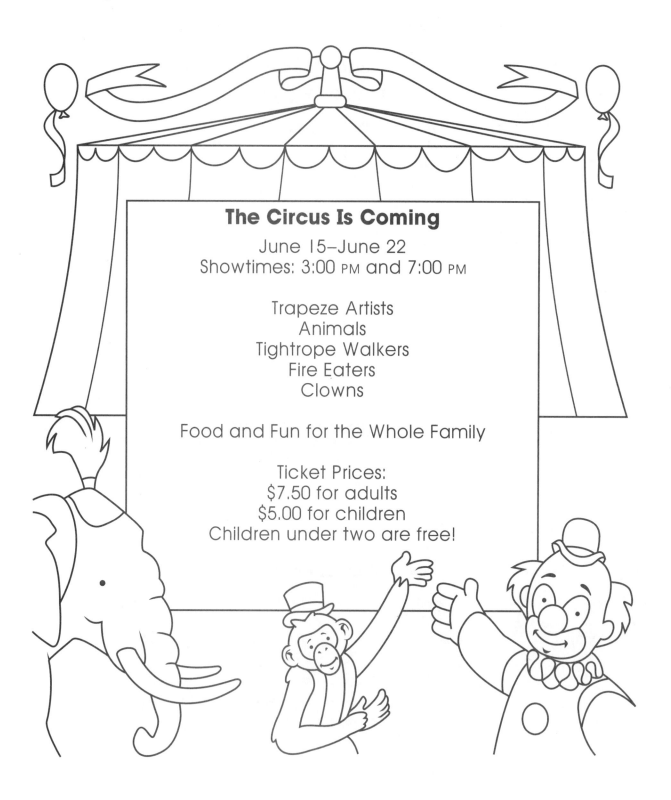

The Circus Is Coming

June 15–June 22
Showtimes: 3:00 PM and 7:00 PM

Trapeze Artists
Animals
Tightrope Walkers
Fire Eaters
Clowns

Food and Fun for the Whole Family

Ticket Prices:
$7.50 for adults
$5.00 for children
Children under two are free!

Use the flyer on page 70 to answer the questions.

1. What is the flyer about?

   A. Clowns are funny.

   B. Have fun with your family.

   C. The circus is coming.

2. Draw a line between the person and how much it costs the person to go to the circus.

   adults $5.00

   children   free

   children two and under $7.50

3. Write an X by the details that are true.

   _____ The circus will be in town on June 20.

   _____ There will be clowns at the circus.

   _____ There are no tightrope walkers at the circus.

   _____ You can see the circus at either 3:00 or 7:00.

   _____ Children under two should not come to the circus.

Sentences tell a complete thought. Write an S if it is a sentence. Write an N if it is not a sentence.

4. _____ The circus is coming to town.

5. _____ Food and fun for the whole family.

6. _____ Children under two are free.

7. _____ The greatest show around.

Read the party invitation.

Come to a Spy Birthday Party

Your **mission**, if you choose to **accept** it. . .

For: Josh's 9th Birthday

When: Saturday, September 13

Time: 4:00–6:00

Where: Papa's Pizza Palace

RSVP by September 10
Call: 555-0145

Use the party invitation on page 72 to answer the questions.

1. Whom is the party for?_____

2. What is the party for? _____

3. When is the party? _____

4. Where is the party?_____

5. By what date should you RSVP? _____

Circle the answer that tells the meaning of each word as used in the invitation. Use a dictionary if you need to.

6. *mission*

    A. old church building

    B. to do church work in other lands

    C. a job that must be done

7. *accept*

    A. to answer "yes"

    B. to agree with

    C. to view as normal

An *apostrophe* (') is used to show a possessive or a contraction. Write a *P* if the apostrophe shows the possessive. Write a *C* if the apostrophe is in a contraction.

8. _____ you're

9. _____ here's

10. _____ Josh's

11. _____ Papa's Pizza Palace

Read the letter.

June 5, 2007

Dear Grandma and Grandpa,

What's happening? I'm just hanging out. Today is the first day of my summer vacation. I have some radical things planned this summer. Later on today, my friend Michael is coming over. We're going to ride our bikes. Tomorrow, I start swimming lessons. Mom said that in two weeks we are going to visit you. I can't wait. Can we go to the park with the water slides? I had a blast last year when we went there. Also, I want to go fishing with Grandpa. This year I'm going to catch the biggest fish. You'll have to buy a new pan to cook it in because I don't think the pans you have are big enough. Well, I have to split. Catch you later.

Love, Nick

DEAR GRANDMA AND GRANDPA

Use the letter on page 74 to answer the questions.

1. Who is the letter to? _____

2. Who is the letter from? _____

3. Name two things that Nick is going to do this summer. _____

_____

Language between friends and family often includes slang words and phrases. *Slang* words are informal words that should not be used in formal speech or writing. Draw a line to connect each slang word to its meaning.

4.	What's happening?	go
5.	hanging out	See you soon.
6.	blast	How are you?
7.	split	relaxing
8.	Catch you later.	fun

Write the two words that make up each contraction.

9. what's _____ _____

10. I'm _____ _____

11. we're _____ _____

12. can't _____ _____

13. you'll _____ _____

14. I'll _____ _____

THE MOUSE AND HIS FOOD

Read the story.

One day, a little mouse sat inside his little house inside a log. "Oh dear," said the mouse. "I have nothing to eat but this small seed. Surely, I will starve." So, the little mouse went out to find some food.

Soon, the little mouse found two acorns. He took the acorns to his house. "Oh dear," said the mouse. "I have nothing to eat but a small seed and these two acorns. What if rain comes and washes them away? Surely, I will starve." So, the little mouse went out to find more food.

Soon, he found a corncob and a piece of cheese. He took them back to his house. "Oh dear," said the mouse. "I have nothing to eat but a small seed, these two acorns, this corncob, and a piece of cheese. Surely, I will starve." So, the little mouse went out to find more food.

Soon, he found six walnuts. He took the walnuts back to his house. "Oh dear," said the mouse. "I have nothing to eat but a small seed, these two acorns, this corncob, a piece of cheese, and these six walnuts. What if snow comes and freezes them all? Surely, I will starve." So, the little mouse went out to find more food.

This went on for days. Finally, the mouse had gathered more food than 10 mice could eat in a year. Soon, rain, wind, and snow did come. But, none of the food was washed away. None of the food blew away. And none of the food froze. But, because the mouse could not eat all of the food, the food rotted.

READING SUCCESS RB-904110

THE MOUSE AND HIS FOOD

Use the story on page 76 to answer the questions.

1. What word best describes the mouse?

   A. friendly

   B. hungry

   C. fearful

2. What happened to the mouse's food?

   A. It blew away.

   B. It rotted.

   C. The mouse ate it.

Homophones are words that sound the same but have different meanings and can have different spellings. Write a word from the story that is a homophone.

3. won _____

4. daze _____

5. deer _____

6. blue _____

7. sum _____

8. sew _____

9. too _____

10. rein _____

Write the plural of each word.

11. mouse _____

12. acorn _____

13. house _____

14. year _____

15. day _____

16. corncob _____

THE ANTS AND THE COOKIES

Read the story.

One day, two ants went exploring. They came across two giant cookies.

"These cookies are huge!" said the first ant.

"One of these cookies would feed my whole family for a month," said the second ant. "But, how can such little ants like us carry such big cookies like these?"

"It seems impossible!" said the first little ant. "But, I must try."

So, the first little ant started to tug and pull at one cookie. Suddenly, a tiny piece broke off the cookie.

"I am going to take this piece back to my family," said the first little ant.

"You go ahead," said the second little ant. "I'm not going to waste my time on such a small piece of cookie. I will find a way to take the whole cookie back to my family."

So, the first ant went home with her small piece of cookie. Soon, the first ant returned. She found the second ant still pushing and shoving the other cookie, but she was unable to move it. Again, the first little ant broke off a small piece of cookie and took it back to her family. This went on for most of the day. The first little ant kept carrying small pieces of cookie back to her family until the entire cookie had been moved. The second little ant finally tired of trying to complete a task that seemed too big to do. She went home with nothing.

THE ANTS AND THE COOKIES

Use the story on page 78 to answer the questions.

1. How did the first little ant carry the cookie home?

    A. She dragged it.

    B. She carried a little bit at a time.

    C. She ate most of it first.

2. What happened to the second little ant?

    A. She got tired of trying and quit.

    B. She carried the cookie home.

    C. She ate the cookie.

Synonyms are words that mean the same or almost the same thing. Draw a line to connect each pair of synonyms.

3. giant   whole

4. tug   move

5. tiny   huge

6. budge   shove

7. entire   little

8. push   pull

Write the past tense for each action word.

9. come _____   10. say _____

11. feed _____   12. take _____

13. start _____   14. move _____

15. go _____   16. break _____

Read the story.

A long time ago, there lived an old woman and an old man. They did not have much money. But, they did have a fine cottage and enough food to eat. One day, they went fishing. They sat on the shore for hours without one bite. Suddenly, the man felt a tug on his line. He reeled in a fish. What a big fish it was! Surely, this fish would feed him and his wife for an entire week. But, as he began to unhook the fish, the fish spoke!

"Please, let me go," said the fish. "If you do, I will grant you three wishes."

"A talking fish!" shouted the old man. "How can this be?" And, without thinking, he threw the fish back into the water.

The old woman shouted, "You foolish man! You threw the fish back without making any wishes. And, you threw back a fish that could feed us for a week. Just once, I wish you would think!"

Just as the words came out of the woman's mouth, a thought popped in the man's mind. "Well," said the man, "your wish has come true. I am thinking. I am thinking that you are a rude woman, and I wish you would keep quiet!"

And, just as the man wished, the woman's mouth was shut tight. The old couple sat and stared at each other. "What have we done?" the man said. "With three wishes, we could have wished for money, food, or fame, but instead we wished away our wishes. Now, the only sensible wish would be that my wife's mouth would be opened."

And, as quickly as the man said the last wish, the woman's mouth was opened. "We don't have more money, food, or fame, but we do have each other. That is enough," said the old man. Together, the old woman and the old man walked back to their cottage.

Use the story on page 80 to answer the questions.

1. What is the moral of the story?

    A. Be careful not to catch talking fish.

    B. Think before you speak.

    C. Always be ready with three wishes.

2. How would you describe the people in the middle of the story?

    A. grumpy

    B. true

    C. silly

Write _T_ for the things that are true. Write _F_ for the things that are false.

3. _____ A long time ago, there lived an old man and an old woman.

4. _____ The couple went fishing.

5. _____ The man caught a talking fish.

6. _____ The woman's mouth shut tight.

7. _____ The couple walked back to their house.

Add correct punctuation to the end of each sentence.

8. Have you ever seen a talking fish

9. That fish can talk

10. My dad caught a fish

11. Can you go fishing with me

Read the story.

One day, an old woman decided to bake gingerbread in the shape of a boy. She used raisins for his eyes and licorice for his mouth. She used cinnamon candies for the buttons on his vest. When she was satisfied, she put her little gingerbread boy in the oven. Soon, she could smell the delicious scent of warm gingerbread. She opened the oven door, and the little gingerbread boy popped out.

"Yum. You smell delicious," sighed the old woman.

"Run, run, as fast as you can. You can't catch me. I'm too fast, you see!" the gingerbread boy laughed, and then he ran away.

"Oh my," screamed the old woman, and she ran after her little gingerbread boy.

The little gingerbread boy came to a young boy. "Yum. You smell delicious," shouted the boy.

But, the gingerbread boy just laughed and said, "Run, run, as fast as you can. You can't catch me. I'm too fast, you see!" And, the little gingerbread boy ran away with the old woman and the boy close behind.

Soon, the gingerbread boy came to a man. "Yum. You smell delicious," bellowed the man.

But, the gingerbread boy just laughed and said, "Run, run, as fast as you can. You can't catch me. I'm too fast, you see!" And, the gingerbread boy ran away with the old woman, the boy, and the man close behind.

Soon, the gingerbread boy came to a river. "Oh dear," cried the gingerbread boy. "How will I cross this river?"

"I'll give you a ride," snickered an alligator with a sly smile. "Just jump on my back."

The gingerbread boy accepted the alligator's offer. As you might expect, the gingerbread boy did not make it across the river but instead made it into the belly of the alligator.

When the old woman, the boy, and the man came to the river, they knew what had happened. "Let's go home," sighed the old woman. "I will make some gingerbread for us, just a plain loaf of gingerbread."

Use the story on page 82 to answer the questions.

1. Number the events from the story in order.

   _____ The old woman said she would bake a plain loaf of gingerbread.

   _____ The old woman chased the gingerbread boy.

   _____ The old woman made gingerbread in the shape of a boy.

   _____ The boy chased the gingerbread boy.

   _____ The man chased the gingerbread boy.

Use the recipe to answer the questions.

Gingerbread Cookies

1 cup molasses	1/2 cup brown sugar	1/3 cup shortening
1/3 cup water	1 tsp. baking soda	1 tsp. cinnamon
6 cups flour	2 tsp. ginger	1 tsp. allspice

1. Mix together molasses, brown sugar, water, and shortening.
2. Sift together flour, soda, and spices. Then, add to molasses mixture. Cover and refrigerate overnight.
3. Heat oven to 350°. Roll out dough on a floured board. Use cookie cutters to cut shapes. Place cookies on a cookie sheet. Bake 10–12 minutes.

Makes 2 dozen cookies.

2. How many cups of flour are needed? _____

3. How hot should the oven be? _____

4. How long should the dough be refrigerated? _____

5. How long should the cookies bake? _____

6. How many cookies will this recipe make? _____

PICKLED POTATO PANCAKES

Read the story.

Once upon a time, in a kingdom far away, there lived a prince named Peter. Prince Peter had a pony named Pepper. Pepper would eat only pickled potato pancakes. One day, the royal kitchen ran out of pickled potato pancakes.

"What will we do?," shouted the prince.

"I will search throughout the land," declared the prince's faithful servant, Patrick. "I will not return until I find some pickled potato pancakes."

Needless to say, it was not easy to find such a food. Patrick searched far and wide. He explored kingdom after kingdom. But, no pickled potato pancakes were to be found. One day, Patrick came upon a castle deep within the forest. The castle was painted a pleasant shade of pink. In this castle lived a beautiful princess. Her name was Penelope. Penelope lived alone with her pet pig named Porky. Patrick was hungry from his long journey. So, Patrick approached the pink castle that belonged to Princess Penelope.

"May I have a bite to eat?" questioned Patrick.

The princess giggled. "I'm sorry," said the princess, "but the only thing I know how to make is pickled potato pancakes. It's all my Porky will eat."

Now, it was Patrick's turn to laugh. "You are just what I am looking for," chuckled Patrick. Patrick told the princess his story and asked her if she would come back to the castle with him.

"Sure, we'll come," agreed Penelope.

When Princess Penelope, Patrick, and Porky arrived back at the castle, it was love at first sight between the prince and princess. They lived happily ever after, making pickled potato pancakes for Prince Peter's pony, Pepper, and Princess Penelope's pig, Porky.

PICKLED POTATO PANCAKES

Use the story on page 84 to answer the questions.

1. All fairy tales are *fantasy*, or make-believe. Put an *X* by the things that make this story a fairy tale.

    _____ Once upon a time, in a kingdom far away. . .

    _____ Prince Peter had a pony named Pepper.

    _____ Pepper ate only pickled potato pancakes.

    _____ Patrick was hungry from his long journey.

    _____ The castle was painted a pleasant shade of pink.

    _____ They lived happily ever after.

Synonyms are words that mean the same or almost the same thing. Draw a line to connect each pair of synonyms.

2. searched   laughed

3. giggled   hunted

4. declared   questioned

5. beautiful   pretty

6. asked   proclaimed

Alliteration means using the same beginning sounds. For each word, write two more words that start like the word.

7. bear   _____   _____

8. dog   _____   _____

9. turtle   _____   _____

Read the story.

In a kingdom far away lived a **frugal** king. Each week, the king put some of his kingdom's food into a large storehouse in the castle. The people of the kingdom were not happy.

"Why does the king take our food and store it away?" asked one of the townspeople.

"I bet that he is taking our food and eating it himself," accused another.

"We are starving," sighed another. "We barely have enough to eat."

"All of the people in the kingdom on the other side of the land eat until their stomachs almost burst," shouted another. "Our king is cruel to his people."

Despite what the townspeople said, the king kept taking a portion of the food and storing it away.

One day, a **famine** came to the land. It was impossible to grow wheat to make bread. It was impossible to feed the cows, so there was no milk or cheese, and the famine grew worse. The townspeople in kingdoms throughout the land were hungry. But, the people from the frugal king's kingdom had plenty to eat. The king opened the doors of the storehouse and fed his people. The townspeople knew that the king's frugality had saved their lives.

Use the story on page 86 to answer the questions.

1. How did the people feel about the king at the beginning of the story?

   A. They were proud of the king.

   B. They thought that the king was mean and selfish.

   C. They thought that the king was fat.

2. How did the people feel about the king at the end of the story?

   A. They thought that the king was mean and selfish.

   B. They thought that the king was rich.

   C. They were grateful to the king.

Use the verb *is* with a singular subject. Use the verb *are* with a plural subject. Write *is* or *are* to complete each sentence.

3. The king _____ frugal.

4. We _____ starving.

5. They _____ working hard.

6. The townspeople _____ complaining.

7. The boy _____ hungry.

8. What does the word *frugal* mean?

   A. mean

   B. careful

   C. selfish

9. What does the word *famine* mean?

   A. a wild beast

   B. food shortage

   C. special holiday

READING SUCCESS RB-904110

THE SWING

Read the poem.

How do you like to go up in a swing,
Up in the air so blue?
Oh, I do think it the pleasantest thing
Ever a child can do!

Up in the air and over the wall,
Till I can see so wide,
Rivers and trees and cattle and all
Over the countryside—

Till I look down on the garden green,
Down on the roof so brown—
Up in the air I go flying again,
Up in the air and down!

Robert Louis Stevenson

READING SUCCESS RB-904110   © Rainbow Bridge Publishing

THE SWING

Use the poem on page 88 to answer the questions.

1. Draw a line to match each color word to the thing it describes.

   blue   roof

   green   air

   brown   garden

2. This poem has the rhythm of a swing going back and forth. Read the poem aloud to someone else. Try to read it with the rhythm of the swing.

Prepositions are words like *up* and *down* that tell position. Circle the preposition in each sentence.

3. The balloon sailed into the clouds.

4. The ball landed on the roof.

5. The girl jumped over the wall.

6. The little boy ran down the stairs.

7. The dog is in the house.

Draw a line to connect each pair of rhyming words.

8. down   do

9. blue   swing

10. all   brown

11. thing   wall

The suffix *est* means most. Add *est* to each word below.

12. big _____

13. nice _____

14. long _____

15. little _____

16. pretty _____

Read the story.

Kate loves doing things with her dad. He is her best friend. Her dad loves to play basketball. He is on a team. Kate loves to play basketball. She is on a team, too. Her dad is the coach of her team. Sometimes after a game, Kate and her dad go out for ice cream. They both have chocolate fudge ice cream.

Sometimes before dinner, Kate and her dad go for a run. They run around the track at the neighborhood school. Kate enjoys running with her dad. Sometimes, they talk when they run. Sometimes, they just run.

At bedtime, Kate's dad always tucks her in. He tells her stories. Her favorite stories are about when her dad was a little boy. Next, her dad talks with her about what happened during the day. Then, he kisses her gently on the forehead. Kate thinks her dad is the greatest.

Use the story on page 90 to answer the questions.

1. What is this story about?

   A. having fun

   B. why Kate loves her dad

   C. eating ice cream

2. *Inferred* means something isn't told exactly, but you get the idea from what is said. Read the sentences below. Write *S* if the sentence is stated in the story. Write *I* if the sentence is inferred in the story. Write *U* if the sentence is unknown.

   _____ Kate's dad plays on a basketball team.

   _____ Kate's mom plays on a basketball team, too.

   _____ Kate's dad loves her.

   _____ Kate has a little brother.

   _____ Kate's dad always tucks her in.

   _____ Kate and her dad like to talk.

Write the plural of each word.

3. story _____

4. cone _____

5. kiss _____

6. team _____

7. hug _____

8. boy _____

9. friend _____

10. girl _____

Read the story.

Hannah Hippo wanted to be big. But Hannah was the smallest hippo in the river. One day, Hannah looked at her reflection in the river. "Look at my teeth. My teeth are big! So, I must be big."

Soon, a bird came to the river. "I am big, and I have big teeth," said Hannah. "Yes, you are big," said the bird as it flew away.

Next, a turtle came to the river. "I am big, and I have big teeth," said Hannah. "Yes, you are big," said the turtle as he sauntered away.

Before long, a baby tiger came to the river. "I am big, and I have big teeth," said Hannah. "Yes, you are big," said the baby tiger as he scampered away.

Hannah sat by the river for a long time. "I am big, and I have big teeth. But this is no fun. I have no one to play with." Soon, Hannah's mom and dad came to the river. Hannah looked at her mom and dad. Hannah looked at their big teeth. Hannah felt small. But Hannah did not mind. At least she had someone to play with. Maybe being small was not so bad after all.

READING SUCCESS RB-904110 © Rainbow Bridge Publishing

WHAT'S BIG?

Use the story on page 92 to answer the questions.

1. What did Hannah Hippo want?

    A. for her mom and dad to leave her alone

    B. to be big

    C. to fly like a bird

2. Number the events from the story in order.

    _____ Soon, a bird came to the river.

    _____ Hannah Hippo wanted to be big.

    _____ Hannah's mom and dad came to the river.

    _____ Next, a turtle came to the river.

3. Write a *B* if the animal is bigger than Hannah. Write an *S* if the animal is smaller than Hannah.

    _____ the turtle

    _____ Hannah's mom

    _____ the bird

    _____ all of the hippos in the river

Add *er* or *est* to the word to complete each sentence.

4. Between a tiger, a bird, and a turtle, a bird is the small_____.

5. Hannah was the small_____ hippo in the river.

6. A bird is small_____ than a turtle.

7. Hannah was small_____ than her dad.

Read the story.

My mother baked a gigantic cookie for me. I sat on my porch to eat it. But, before I took a bite, my friend Anna came by.

"Will you share your cookie with me?" Anna asked. I broke my cookie into two pieces, one for me and one for Anna. But, before we took a bite, Jesse and Lucy came by.

"Will you share your cookie with us?" they asked. Anna and I each broke our cookie pieces into two more pieces. Now, we had four pieces: one for me, one for Anna, one for Jesse, and one for Lucy. But, before we took a bite, four more friends came by.

"Will you share your cookie with us?" they asked. Anna, Jesse, Lucy, and I all broke our pieces in half. Now, we had enough to share between eight friends. But, before we took a bite, eight more friends came by.

"Will you share your cookie with us?" they asked. We all broke our pieces in half to share with our eight new friends. I looked at my gigantic cookie. It was no longer gigantic.

"Hey, does anyone know what is gigantic when there's one, but small when there are sixteen?" I asked.

"No, what?" my friends asked.

"My cookie," I laughed.

© Rainbow Bridge Publishing

Use the story on page 94 to answer the questions.

1. What happened to the cookie?

    A. It was shared between friends.

    B. It broke in half.

    C. It ran away.

2. Number the events from the story in order.

    _____ Jesse and Lucy came by.

    _____ Mother baked a cookie.

    _____ Anna came by.

    _____ Four friends came by.

    _____ Eight friends came by.

3. Circle the words that mean the same as *gigantic*.

    big   huge   enormous   delicious   large   tiny

4. Write three words that are antonyms (opposite) of *gigantic*.

    _____   _____   _____

Add correct punctuation to the end of each sentence.

5. My mother baked a cookie for me

6. Will you share your cookie with me

7. Do you like chocolate chip cookies

8. My favorite cookie is a snickerdoodle

9. How can we divide the cookie between three people

THE RIGHT PET

Read the story.

"Please, Mom. May I please have a pet of my own?" asked Jackie.

"Well, you have shown that you can be responsible. I guess that it's time you had your own pet," said Mother.

"Hurray! Let's go!" shouted Jackie.

"But, first, you need to think about the right pet," said Mother.

"The right pet? I don't understand," said Jackie.

"The right pet is the right one for you. The right pet is the right size. You need to think about where you will keep your pet. You need to think about how much time you have to take care of it," explained Mother.

"Well," said Jackie. "We live in an apartment, so I guess that it will need to be small. I want a pet that I can hold. I want a pet that I can cuddle with."

"Now, you're thinking," said Mother. "Let's go see what we can find."

Jackie and her mom went to the pet store. Jackie said to the pet store owner, "I am looking for a small, furry pet that I can hold." The pet store owner showed Jackie a puppy. The puppy was small and furry. But, Jackie knew that it would not always be small and furry. It would grow up to be a big dog. Jackie looked at a goldfish. "No good," she said. "I can't hold it." Finally, Jackie saw a hamster.

"This is perfect. It is small. I can hold it. It has fur. I can cuddle with it. This is the right pet for me," said Jackie. Jackie took the pet home. Now, Jackie's only problem was deciding on just the right name for just the right pet.

Use the story on page 96 to answer the questions.

1. What did Jackie want?

    A. a puppy

    B. a pet of her own

    C. something big and furry

2. What did Jackie's mom want her to think about?

    A. the right pet

    B. how much a pet costs

    C. her school work

3. Write an *X* by the things you should think about when choosing a pet.

    _____ the size of the pet

    _____ if the pet is thirsty

    _____ where you will keep the pet

    _____ how much care the pet needs

    _____ if the pet needs a bath

Write the two words that make up each contraction.

4. it's   _____   _____

5. don't   _____   _____

6. it'll   _____   _____

7. I'm   _____   _____

THE PUMPKIN FARM

Read the story.

Every October, Mrs. Lee's class takes a field trip to the pumpkin farm. They walk around the barnyard and through the barn. They see some farm animals. Then, they go for a hayride. A big tractor pulls a large cart of hay. On the hayride, they ride through the apple orchard where the workers are picking apples. Later, they will make applesauce. After the hayride, they go to the pumpkin patch. There are hundreds of pumpkins. Each student picks out a pumpkin to take home. It is always one of the most fun days of the year.

Use the story on page 98 to answer the questions.

1. Which sentence tells the main idea of the story?

    A. There are many things to see and do at a pumpkin farm.

    B. It is fun to choose a pumpkin for Halloween.

    C. Mrs. Lee is a good teacher.

Circle the *verb*, or action word, in each sentence.

2. The children walk through the barn.

3. A big tractor pulls the cart.

4. Each student picks a pumpkin.

5. They ride through the orchard.

6. The children see many animals.

7. Mrs. Lee tells the children about the baby chickens.

8. We laugh at the squealing pigs.

9. The pumpkins grow really big.

Use the bold words to make a compound word. Write the word on the line to complete each sentence.

10. A **ride** in **hay** is called a _____.

11. The **yard** by a **barn** is called a _____.

12. A **sauce** made of **apples** is called _____.

13. A **house** for a **dog** is called a _____.

14. Circle the animals the children may have seen at the farm.

    sheep   horses   giraffes   hippopotamuses   chickens   cows

A TRIP TO THE ZOO

Read the story.

Martha **loves** going to the zoo. She likes to **watch** the flamingos stand on one foot. She likes to watch the giraffes nibble leaves from the trees. Martha thinks that the gorillas are the most fun to watch. The babies like to make faces at Martha. Two of the baby gorillas roll down the hill when they play. Martha wishes that she could roll down the hill with them.

When she grows up, Martha wants to work at the zoo. She wants to help take care of the animals. Until then, she will look forward to her next trip to the zoo!

Use the story on page 100 to answer the questions.

1. Which sentence tells the main idea of the story?

    A. Martha loves going to the zoo.

    B. Martha loves watching gorillas.

    C. Martha loves to take a vacation.

2. Which animal does Martha like to watch the most?

    A. flamingo

    B. giraffe

    C. gorilla

3. Draw a line to connect each animal to the thing it does in the story.

    baby gorilla   nibbles leaves

    giraffe   rolls down the hill

    flamingo   stands on one foot

4. Why does Martha want to work at the zoo when she grows up?

    A. to get in the zoo for free

    B. to earn some money

    C. to care for the animals

5. What does *loves* mean in the story?

    A. has feelings for

    B. enjoys

    C. wants

6. What does *watch* mean in the story?

    A. to observe

    B. a timepiece

    C. to guard

Read the story.

Today, our class took a field trip to the fire station. First, we met Captain Jim. He showed us the big fire trucks. The fire trucks, or fire engines, have many switches and valves. They have many compartments that hold the equipment and tools used to fight fires and help in emergencies.

We saw the large hoses the firefighters use to extinguish, or put out fires. We saw the tall ladders the firefighters climb to reach high places. We saw the uniforms the firefighters wear when they fight fires. We got to try on their coats, pants, boots, and hats. The clothes firefighters wear are big and heavy. Frankie fell over because of the weight of the clothes.

Then, Captain Jim showed us where the firefighters live when they are on duty. Inside the fire station, there are beds, showers, and a kitchen. The firefighters take turns cooking meals and shopping for food.

Suddenly, we heard a loud siren. The siren meant that there was an emergency. Captain Jim and the other firefighters quickly jumped on their fire trucks and drove away. It was interesting to see the fire station and learn about the job of a firefighter.

Use the story on page 102 to answer the questions.

1. Which sentence tells the main idea of the story?

    A. Firefighters work hard.

    B. Firefighters live at the fire station.

    C. Our class visited a fire station.

2. Number the events from the story in order.

    _____ The firefighters jumped on their fire trucks and drove away.

    _____ We saw the big fire trucks.

    _____ We heard a loud siren.

    _____ We put on the firefighters' coats, pants, boots, and hats.

Write the letter of the word or words to match the word that has the same or about the same meaning.

3. _____ big

4. _____ extinguish

5. _____ uniform

6. _____ tall

7. _____ equipment

A. put out

B. special clothes

C. tools

D. large

E. high

Read the story.

Mother thought the trip to the grocery store was a chore. Danielle thought the trip to the grocery store was an adventure. Mother could see only the things on her list. Danielle saw the variety of things to eat.

In the produce department, Danielle counted nine different types of apples. Danielle's mother picked up one bag of Granny Smith apples. They were the type of apples she always bought. They were the family's favorite.

The cereal aisle was like a library filled with colorful books. Danielle enjoyed reading all of the different names. She enjoyed reading about all of the different prizes inside the boxes. Danielle's mother just found the family-size box of their favorite cereal. Danielle noted that it was one of the few cereals without sugar. Danielle wondered how her mother always managed to find the one box of cereal without sugar.

In the dairy section, Danielle wondered how many cows it took to fill all of the containers of milk. She wondered if the cows that gave low-fat milk were skinnier than the cows that gave the whole milk. Danielle's mother always chose two gallons of low-fat milk. Once in a while, if Danielle's mother was in a particularly good mood, she would toss some yogurt into the cart.

At the checkout stand, Danielle loved to count all of the different types of gum. She wondered who would chew all of the gum. Danielle's mother just worried about having enough money to pay for the groceries. For her mother, going to the grocery store was a chore. For Danielle, it was an adventure!

A TRIP TO THE GROCERY STORE

Divide the following words into syllables. Use a dictionary if you need help.

1. adventure _____

2. different _____

3. favorite _____

4. department _____

5. colorful _____

6. container _____

7. variety _____

8. particularly _____

Write the base word for each word.

9. reading _____

10. colorful _____

11. noted _____

12. managed _____

13. skinnier _____

14. worried _____

BRIAUNA'S FAVORITE PLACE

Read the story.

Briauna lives in Newfoundland, Canada. Today, she is visiting her favorite place, a high cliff that overlooks the ocean. She likes to watch the fishing boats bob like corks in the blue water. She listens to the cries of the seagulls as they look for food. She admires the beauty of the tall lighthouse. She laughs as she watches the whales play. Briauna lies on her back. She sees animals in the clouds. Briauna loves to feel the mist from the ocean against her face. It is a peaceful day.

Suddenly, a huge wave crashes onto the shore. The fishing boats start coming to port as fast as they can. The clouds darken. A strong wind begins to blow. A foghorn cries out. It warns the sailors that a storm is coming. The waves get bigger and bigger.

As the storm comes in, Briauna is glad that she is high above the angry ocean. She takes one last look at the beautiful white-capped waves. Then, she runs home.

Use the story on page 106 to answer the questions.

1. Which sentence tells the main idea of the story?

    A. Briauna visits her favorite place.

    B. There are sailors and whales.

    C. The weather changes.

2. What did the fishing boats look like on the ocean?

    A. bobbing corks

    B. sinking ships

    C. specks in the sea

3. Why did the foghorn cry out?

    A. to help the seagulls find food

    B. to tell the whales where the fishing boats were

    C. to warn the sailors about the storm

Write the two words that make up each compound word.

4. overlooks _____ _____

5. seagulls _____ _____

6. lighthouse _____ _____

7. foghorn _____ _____

Adjectives **are words that describe nouns. Write the adjective from the story that describes each noun.**

8. _____ water   9. _____ wave

10. _____ day   11. _____ wind

HOW TO FROST A CAKE

Read the story.

Jessica is making a cake for her mother's birthday. Her grandmother helped her bake the cake. But, her grandmother had to go home. She left the following directions for Jessica:

1. When the cake is cool, remove it from the baking pan and put it on a plate. To do this, place a plate face down on the cake. Then, flip the cake and the plate over. Remove the baking pan.
2. Open the can of frosting. Spoon some frosting onto the middle of the cake.
3. Spread the frosting using the spreader. Always work from the center out to the sides. Add more frosting as needed. Spread the frosting evenly over all of the cake.

Be careful not to press too hard, or you will tear the cake.

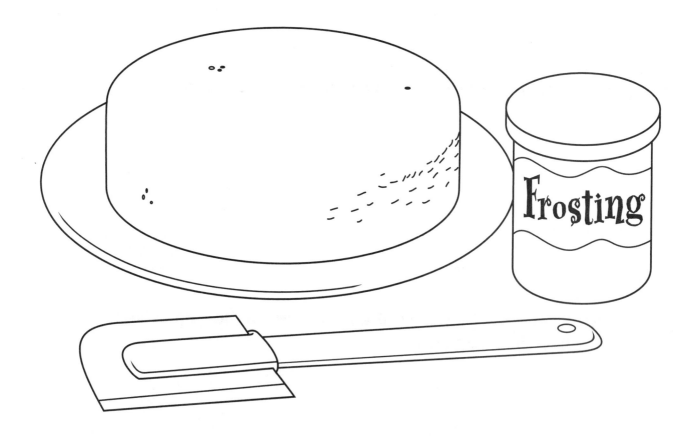

HOW TO FROST A CAKE

Use the story on page 108 to answer the questions.

1. Which sentence tells the main idea of the story?

    A. Making a birthday cake is hard.

    B. Jessica wanted to be a good cook.

    C. Jessica wanted to help make a birthday cake.

2. What warning did Grandma give Jessica?

    A. Don't lick your fingers.

    B. Don't use too much frosting.

    C. Be careful not to press too hard.

3. What is the meaning of the word *directions* in this story?

    A. north, south, east, and west

    B. steps to finish the cake by frosting it

    C. a map to someone's house

Use the recipe to answer the questions.

Vanilla Frosting
>   3 cups powdered sugar
>   1/3 cup butter, softened
>   1 tsp. vanilla
>   1 tbsp. milk
>   1. Mix butter and sugar together. Stir in vanilla and milk. Beat until smooth.
>   2. Spread on cake.

Makes enough frosting for one 13 inch x 9 inch cake.

---

4. How many cups of powered sugar do you need? _____

5. Do you need more milk or more vanilla? _____

6. How long should you beat the frosting? _____

Read the story.

"Happy Mother's Day," Nathan said. Nathan gave his mother a large box with a pretty bow.

"What is it?" his mother asked.

"You have to guess," Nathan said. "I'll give you a hint. It's soft and blue."

"Can I wear it?" asked his mother.

"Yes," said Nathan.

"I think I know," his mother said. She opened the box. "Thank you! It is just what I asked for," she said.

Nathan's mother took the gift out of the box. She put it on over her head. She put her arms in the sleeves. It fit just right. Nathan's mother gave him a big hug.

Use the story on page 110 to answer the questions.

1. Why did Nathan give his mother a present?

    A. It was Mother's Day.

    B. It was her birthday.

    C. His mother had been sick.

2. What did Mother give Nathan?

    A. a present

    B. a hug

    C. a sweater

Homophones are words that sound the same but have different meanings and can have different spellings. Draw a line between each pair of homophones.

3. wear   ewe

4. him   blew

5. you   where

6. blue   no

7. know   hymn

The words *it*, *she*, and *he* take the place of a person or thing in a sentence. Answer the questions about these sentences.

8. He gave her a large box. Who is *he*? _____

9. She opened the box. Who is *she*? _____

10. She put it on over her head. What is *it*? _____

THE BIRTHDAY PRESENT MIX-UP

Read the story. Then, fill in the table.

Today is Rachel's birthday. She invited four friends to her party. Each friend brought a present. Rachel's little brother mixed up the tags on the presents. Can you use these clues to put the tags on the right presents?

Kelly's present has flowered wrapping paper and a bow.

Kate's present is square and has a bow.

Meg forgot the bow on her present.

Lisa's present has striped wrapping paper.

Write an *X* in the box when you know a present was not brought by the girl. Write an *O* when you know a present was brought by the girl.

Kate				
Kelly				
Lisa				
Meg				

READING SUCCESS RB-904110

THE BIRTHDAY PRESENT MIX-UP

Use the story on page 112 to answer the questions.

1. What event is happening in the story?

   A. Rachel's birthday party

   B. Meg's birthday party

   C. Friendship Day

2. Write *T* for the things that are true. Write *F* for the things that are false.

   _____ Kate's present has a bow.

   _____ Meg's present has a bow.

   _____ Kelly's present has striped wrapping paper.

   _____ Lisa forgot to bring a present.

   _____ Rachel's little brother was helpful at the party.

An *apostrophe* (') is used to show possession. Circle the word that needs an apostrophe in each sentence. Write the word correctly on the line.

3. Rachels brother is three years old. _____

4. Kates present has a big bow. _____

5. My brothers friend spent the night. _____

6. Each presents tag was missing. _____

7. Lisas present has striped paper. _____

Read the story. Then, fill in the table.

Today is the neighborhood pet show. Holly, Amanda, Nico, and Nathan have brought their pets. Can you match each child to the child's pet?

Nathan's pet likes to chase the girl's cat.

Holly's pet sings from its perch.

Nico's pet runs around on a wheel in its cage.

Write an *X* in the box when you know the pet does not belong to a child. Write an *O* when you know the pet does belong to the child.

Holly				
Amanda				
Nico				
Nathan				

Use the story on page 114 to answer the questions.

1. What event is happening in the story?

   A. school fair

   B. pet show

   C. circus

2. Draw a line to connect each pet to its owner.

   Holly   cat

   Amanda   dog

   Nico   hamster

   Nathan   bird

3. Write the type of pet next to what it does.

   A. sings from its perch   _____

   B. runs on a wheel in its cage _____

   C. chases the cat   _____

4. Write an X by each animal that would not make a good pet.

   _____ elephant

   _____ rabbit

   _____ lion

   _____ giraffe

   _____ fish

   _____ dog

WHO'S MY PEN PAL?

Read the story.

For one year, I have been writing to a pen pal. A pen pal is a friend you write letters to. My pen pal's name is Max. He is in the second grade. He lives in Canada with his family. Today, Max is coming for a visit. I am going to meet him at the airport. I have never seen Max, so I'm not sure what he looks like. Max said to look for a boy with light hair and glasses. Max said he would be wearing a baseball cap and carrying a backpack. Can you find Max?

WHO'S MY PEN PAL?

Use the story on page 116 to answer the questions.

1. Circle the picture of Max.

2. What is a pen pal?

   A. a friend you write letters to

   B. a cousin who lives far away

   C. a person from Canada

3. How long has the author been writing to Max?

   A. one month

   B. one year

   C. two years

4. Write *T* for the things that are true. Write *F* for the things that are false. Write *U* for the things that are unknown.

   _____ Max has light hair.

   _____ Max is in the third grade.

   _____ Max has a dog.

   _____ Max wears glasses.

   _____ Max likes to play soccer.

Write the two words that make up each compound word.

5. airport   _____   _____

6. baseball   _____   _____

7. backpack   _____   _____

TREASURE MAP

Read the story.

Ben and Matt were playing pirates. While digging for treasure, they found this map. Follow the directions to find the treasure. Mark an *X* where the treasure is buried.

Start in the Red River Valley.

Go northeast to the Black Forest.

Go northeast to the next forest.

Travel north to the Purple Mountains.

Cross the Red River to the Blue Mountains.

Go south, but do not cross the Red River again.

The treasure is buried here.

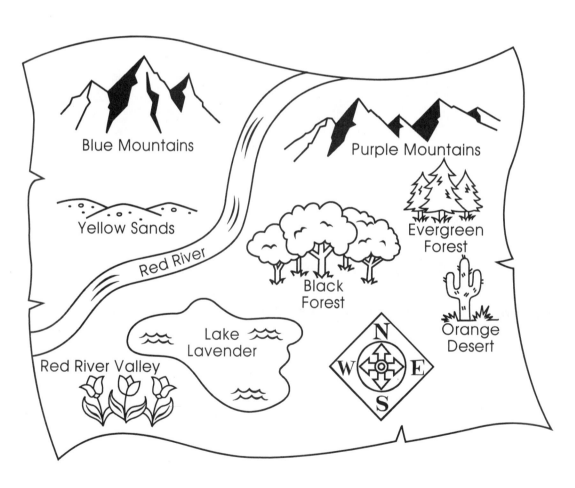

TREASURE MAP

Use the story on page 118 to answer the questions.

1. Where is the treasure buried? _____

2. When you go northeast from the Black Forest, what forest do you find?

   _____

3. Draw a line from the color to the place as noted on the map.

   yellow   mountains

   orange   river

   red   sands

   purple   desert

Write the base word for each word.

4. playing   _____

5. digging   _____

6. buried   _____

7. missing   _____

8. hunting   _____

Cross out the word that does not belong in each group.

9. blue   yellow   red   sky

10. forest   mountains   tree   desert

11. north   left   south   east

12. desert   ocean   river   lake

13. mountain   hill   peak   valley

 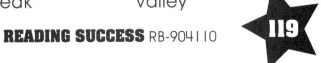

Read the game directions.

Find a friend and play the game.

<u>What You Will Need:</u>

Coin

Game markers

<u>Object of the Game:</u>

To be the first to cross the finish line

<u>How to Play:</u>

The youngest player goes first.

Flip a coin. Move 1 space for heads. Move 2 spaces for tails. Follow the directions on each space you land on.

START →	Slow start. Go back 1 space.	Great start! Go ahead 2 spaces.			Tripped on shoelace. Go back 1 space.	
			Running strong. Take another turn.			
	Record time. Go ahead 3 spaces.		Leg cramps. Lose a turn.			
				Getting tired. Go back 3 spaces.		
	Missed a hurdle. Go back 2 spaces.					FINISH

READING SUCCESS RB-904110

Use the game directions on page 120 to answer the questions.

1. What are the game directions for?

    A. To teach you how to play the game.

    B. To teach you how to run in a race.

    C. To teach you how to come in first place.

2. Draw a line to connect each action with its consequence.

    A. tripped on shoelace   go back 2 spaces

    B. getting tired   win the game

    C. missed a hurdle   go back 1 space

    D. flipped coin is heads   move ahead 1 space

    E. flipped coin is tails   move ahead 2 spaces

    F. cross the finish line   go back 3 spaces

3. Who goes first?

    A. the player who has the game

    B. the biggest player

    C. the youngest player

4. What is the object of the game?

    A. to not trip when running a race

    B. to be the first to cross the finish line

    C. to get the best start

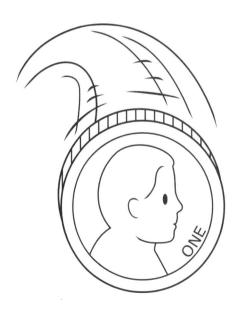

Page 7

1. C.; 2. C.; 3. a computer, DVDs, maps, encyclopedias, a couch; 4. more; Answers will vary.; 5. quietly; Answers will vary.; 6. anyplace; Answers will vary.; 7. be; Answers will vary.

Page 9

1. A.; 2. basketball: winter; soccer: spring; baseball: summer; football: fall; 3. shoot; 4. kick; 5. hit; 6. run; 7. hoop; 8. football; 9. baseball

Page 11

1. 2, 5, 1, 3, 4; 2. snow, man; 3. snow, ball; 4. pine, cone; 5. out, side; 6. days; 7. snowmen; 8. sticks; 9. snowballs; 10. pinecones

Page 13

1. A.; 2. C.; 3. B.; 4. grows: rows; gold: behold; seen: green; along: song; see: me; 5. daisy; 6. buttercup; 7. butterfly

Page 15

1. A.; 2. A.; 3. 26; 4. 15; 5. 31; 6. 19

Page 17

1. B.; 2. sight: storm clouds moving in; touch: tiny sprinkles on my face; taste: little drops inside my mouth; sound: tapping on the window; smell: clean, fresh air; 3. in; 4. chase; 5. inside; 6. know; 7. clean; 8. moving; 9. letting; 10. playing; 11. tapping

Page 19

1. C.; 2. B.; 3. A; 4. B.; 5. A. spring, time; B. blue, bird; C. winter, time; 6. Answers will vary.

Page 21

1. A.; 2. C.; 3. play outside, go swimming, ride a bike, go to the park; 4. sun, shine; 5. out, side; 6. rain, drop

Page 23

1. A.; 2. It is sweet.; The lemonade has a lot of ice.; You have the time.; 3. A.; 4. it, will; 5. it, is; 6. you, have; 7. I, have

Page 25

1. C.; 2. A. big sister; B. Mom; C. Dad; D. little brother; 3. dish: fish; wig: pig; hat: cat; log: dog; 4. "Let's go shopping," said Mother.; 5. "Can we buy a pet?" asked my brother.; 6. "We don't need a pet," said my father.; 7. "That dog needs a home," said my mother.; 8. "Okay," said my father, "we can buy the dog."

Page 27

1. big: little; solid: spots; white: black; fast: slow; 2. o; 3. i; 4. a; 5. a; 6. a lost cat; 7. Rachel; 8. 555-0123

Page 29

1. B.; 2. F; 3. T; 4. F; 5. T; 6. swim; 7. fly; 8. learn; 9. swing; 10. be; 11. have

Page 31

1. C.; 2. kicked; 3. roll; 4. cried; 5. paw; 6. moan; 7. crop; 8. bison

Page 33

1. B.; 2. o; 3. a; 4. u; 5. a; 6. 4, 5, 2, 3, 1; 7. 3, 1, 4, 2, 5; 8. 5, 4, 1, 2, 3

Page 35

1. B.; 2. She got the idea to sell the birdhouses.; She made posters.; She hung the posters around the neighborhood.; 3. make: made; hang: hung; give: gave; build: built; sell: sold; 4. bird•house; 5. beau•ti•ful; 6. busi•ness

Page 37

1. A.; 2. B.; 3. A. robin: in a cherry tree; B. magpie: in a pine tree; C. quail: under a bush; 4. A.; 5. peek; 6. watch; 7. count; 8. place; 9. group; 10. melt

Page 39

1. B.; 2. horse: gallops; kangaroo: hops; duck: waddles; fish: swims; bird: flies; snake: slithers; 3. Moves on two feet: penguin, owl, robin, blue jay; Moves on four feet: deer, cat; Flies: owl, robin, blue jay; Swims: whale, goldfish, penguin

Page 41

1. B.; 2. A.; 3. California, United States, Australia; 4. 5, 1, 6, 3, 4, 2, 7

Page 43

1. B.; 2. An ant can carry things many times its weight.; Ants use feelers to help them find food.; An ant's jaw opens sideways.; 3. A.; 4. an ant; 5. ants

Page 45

1. B.; 2. A.; 3. A.; 4. B.; 5. koalas; 6. marsupials; 7. pouches; 8. babies; 9. leaves

Page 47

1. A.; 2. Wash your hands with soap.; Cover your mouth when you cough or sneeze.; Get plenty of sleep.; Eat healthy meals.; 3. T, T, T, F; 4. i; 5. u

Page 49

1. A.; 2. stamps, an album, tweezers, plastic pages; 3. a stamp collector; 4. collect; 5. interest; 6. dirt; 7. damp

Page 51

1. B.; 2. A.; 3. scrap, book; 4. head, line; 5. some, thing; 6. every, one; 7. cut, out; 8. store; 9. memory; 10. supply; 11. organize

Page 53

1. B.; 2. F; 3. T; 4. T; 5. F; 6. My brother was born November 15, 2001; 7. I like to eat pizza, popcorn, pretzels, and pickles.; 8. My favorite Mercer Mayer books are *There's a Nightmare in My Closet*, *There's an Alligator under My Bed*, and *Terrible Troll.*; 9. The title of the book is *A Boy, a Dog, and a Frog.*; 10. Mercer Mayer's birthday is December 30, 1943.

Page 55

1. A.; 2. Grass: living thing, bends in the wind, small, Mother Nature's gift, you can sit on it, green in color; Tree: living thing, stands straight in the wind, tall, Mother Nature's gift, you can climb it, green in color; 3. bend; 4. short; 5. sit

Page 57

1. A.; 2. B.; 3. Chris: born on December 22, straight brown hair and green eyes, missing two front teeth, a good ballplayer; Will: born on December 22, curly red hair and blue eyes, a good ballplayer; 4. base, teeth, play, braces, both

Page 59

1. C.; 2. sister; 3. brother; 4. sister;
5. brother; 6. brother; 7. sister;
8. read: watch TV; whispesr: shouts;
takes ballet: is in scouts; quiet: loud;
humble: proud

Page 61

1. A.; 2. A.; 3. B.; 4. bear: there; kid:
hid; friend: pretend; bed: Ted; me:
see; 5. I, am; 6. it, is; 7. could, not

Page 63

1. C.; 2. talk: chatter; walk: stroll;
run: dash; 3. whisper; 4. dash;
5. slumber; 6. chuckled; 7. no; 8. It
is an adjective.

Page 65

1. She always says or does the
opposite of what they say or do.;
2. F; 3. F; 4. T; 5. T; 6. south; 7. back;
8. adorable; 9. wet; 10. white; 11. full;
12. began; 13. rode; 14. thought;
15. wanted

Page 67

1. The PTA Challenge; 2. 100%
membership; 3. Ms. Sloan's; 4. Mr.
Colburn's; 5. Miss Casaday's and
Ms. Thomas's; 6. Mrs.: married
woman; Mr.: man; Dr.: doctor, man
or woman; Miss: unmarried woman;
Ms.: woman, married or unmarried;
7. yes; 8. no; 9. yes

Page 69

1. A.; 2. C.; 3. A.; 4. C.; 5. knit;
6. clown; 7. laugh; 8. know; 9. serious

Page 71

1. C.; 2. adults: $7.50; children: $5.00;
children two and under: free; 3. The
circus will be in town on June 20.;
There will be clowns at the circus.;
You can see the circus at either
3:00 or 7:00.; 4. S; 5. N; 6. S; 7. N

Page 73

1. Josh; 2. a birthday; 3. Saturday,
September 13 from 4:00–6:00;
4. Papa's Pizza Palace; 5. September
10; 6. C.; 7. A.; 8. C; 9. C; 10. P; 11. P

Page 75

1. Grandma and Grandpa; 2. Nick;
3. visit grandparents, go fishing,
ride bikes, swim, go to the park;
4. What's happening?: How are
you?; 5. hanging out: relaxing;
6. blast: fun; 7. split: go; 8. Catch
you later.: See you soon.; 9. what,
is; 10. I, am; 11. we, are; 12. can, not;
13. you, will; 14. I, will

Page 77

1. C.; 2. B.; 3. one; 4. days; 5. dear;
6. blew; 7. some; 8. so; 9. two/to;
10. rain; 11. mice; 12. acorns;
13. houses; 14. years; 15. days;
16. corncobs

Page 79

1. B.; 2. A.; 3. giant: huge; 4. tug:
pull; 5. tiny: little; 6. budge: move;
7. entire: whole; 8. push: shove;
9. came; 10. said; 11. fed; 12. took;
13. started; 14. moved; 15. went;
16. broke

Page 81

1. B.; 2. A.; 3. T; 4. T; 5. T; 6. T; 7. T;
8. (?); 9. (!); 10. (.); 11. (?)

Page 83

1. 5, 2, 1, 3, 4; 2. 6; 3. 350 degrees;
4. overnight; 5. 10–12 minutes;
6. two dozen

Page 85

1. Once upon a time, in a kingdom
far away. . .; Pepper ate only pickled
potato pancakes.; The castle was
painted a pleasant shade of pink.;
They lived happily ever after.;
2. searched: hunted; 3. giggled:
laughed; 4. declared: proclaimed;
5. beautiful: pretty; 6. asked:
questioned; 7.–9. Answers will vary.

Page 87

1. B.; 2. C.; 3. is; 4. are; 5. are; 6. are;
7. is; 8. B.; 9. B.

Page 89

1. blue: air; green: garden; brown:
roof; 2. Readings will vary.; 3. into;
4. on; 5. over; 6. down; 7. in; 8. down:
brown; 9. blue: do; 10. all: wall;
11. thing: swing; 12. biggest; 13. nicest;
14. longest; 15. littlest; 16. prettiest

Page 91

1. B.; 2. S, U, I, U, S, I; 3. stories; 4. cones; 5. kisses; 6. teams; 7. hugs; 8. boys; 9. friends; 10. girls

Page 93

1. B.; 2. 2, 1, 4, 3; 3. S, B, S, B; 4. est; 5. est; 6. er; 7. er

Page 95

1. A.; 2. 3, 1, 2, 4, 5; 3. big, huge, enormous, large; 4. Answers will vary.; 5. (.); 6. (?); 7. (?); 8. (.); 9. (?)

Page 97

1. B.; 2. A.; 3. the size of the pet, where you will keep the pet, how much care the pet needs; 4. it, is; 5. do, not; 6. it, will; 7. I, am

Page 99

1. A.; 2. walk; 3. pulls; 4. picks; 5. ride; 6. see; 7. tells; 8. laugh; 9. grow; 10. hayride; 11. barnyard; 12. applesauce; 13. doghouse; 14. sheep, horses, chickens, cows

Page 101

1. A.; 2. C.; 3. baby gorilla: rolls down the hill; giraffe: nibbles leaves; flamingo: stands on one foot; 4. C.; 5. B.; 6. A.

Page 103

1. C.; 2. 4, 1, 3, 2; 3. D; 4. A; 5. B; 6. E; 7. C

Page 105

1. ad•ven•ture; 2. dif•fer•ent; 3. fa•vor•ite; 4. de•part•ment; 5. col•or•ful; 6. con•tain•er; 7. va•ri•e•ty; 8. par•tic•u•lar•ly; 9. read; 10. color; 11. note; 12. manage; 13. skinny; 14. worry

Page 107

1. A.; 2. A.; 3. C.; 4. over, looks; 5. sea, gulls; 6. light, house; 7. fog, horn; 8. blue; 9. huge, bigger, beautiful, white-capped; 10. peaceful; 11. strong

Page 109

1. C.; 2. C.; 3. B.; 4. 3 cups; 5. milk; 6. until smooth

Page 111

1. A.; 2. B.; 3. wear: where; 4. him: hymn; 5. you: ewe; 6. blue: blew; 7. know: no; 8. Nathan; 9. Mother; 10. gift/sweater

Page 112

Kate	O	X	X	X
Kelly	X	O	X	X
Lisa	X	X	X	O
Meg	X	X	O	X

Page 113

1. A.; 2. T, F, F, F, F; 3. Rachel's;
4. Kate's; 5. brother's; 6. present's;
7. Lisa's

Page 114

	cat	dog	hamster	bird
Holly	X	X	X	O
Amanda	O	X	X	X
Nico	X	X	O	X
Nathan	X	O	X	X

Page 115

1. B.; 2. Holly: bird; Amanda: cat;
Nico: hamster; Nathan: dog;
3. A. bird; B. hamster; C. dog;
4. elephant, lion, giraffe

Page 117

1.

2. A.; 3. B.; 4. T, F, U, T, U; 5. air, port;
6. base, ball; 7. back, pack

Page 119

1. Yellow Sands; 2. Evergreen Forest;
3. yellow: sands; orange: desert; red:
river; purple: mountains; 4. play;
5. dig; 6. bury; 7. miss; 8. hunt; 9. sky;
10. tree; 11. left; 12. desert; 13. valley

Page 121

1. A.; 2. A. tripped on shoelace: go
back 1 space; B. getting tired: go
back 3 spaces; C. missed a hurdle:
go back 2 spaces; D. flipped coin
is heads: move ahead 1 space;
E. flipped coin is tails: move ahead
2 spaces; F. cross the finish line: win
the game; 3. C.; 4. B.